HOW TO MOTIVATE
AND PERSUADE PEOPLE

HOW TO MOTIVATE AND PERSUADE PEOPLE

by GABRIEL S. CARLIN

Author of *The Power of Enthusiastic Selling*

PARKER PUBLISHING COMPANY, INC.
West Nyack, New York

Second printing.... January, 1967

PRINTED IN THE UNITED STATES OF AMERICA

42411—B & P

To Rosalind,
Donald, and
Beverly.

PREFACE

This book is designed to help those who want to step into positions of influence, leadership, and responsibility.

It is aimed at the thousands of men and women who are destined to rise to the top of their organizations—business or otherwise.

It will do even more than that. It will serve as a practical guide to personal success in *any* economic or organizational endeavor.

It will, we hope, encourage a reappraisal of yourself and your position. It will provoke some new ideas on how you can become even more successful.

This book is based on a philosophy that puts an unbounding confidence in what man can do.

G. S. C.

CONTENTS

5. *To Cook on All Burners You Must Plan on All Ranges* (Cont.):

not the limit. The basics of planning. Planning is a flexible tool. Anticipate the unexpected. It must be customer oriented. No growth without profits. Precheck the moves.

Get the right people. Know where to look. Interview for results. Tests are tools, not crutches. Look at the entire man. The spots don't change. Pick the stars. Make it worthwhile. You might already have him.

Let George do it. Determine what really needs to be done. Find the George who can do it. Train him to do it. Let him do the job.

Don't abdicate. Lighten the load for higher flight. You are not a switchboard or the neck of a bottle. Stay on top of the job. Assure the payoff. Set the stage. Don't assume. Correct the mistakes.

Set the course and guide the ship. The laws of leadership. What subordinates expect. Let them grow. Control the pressure. For power or progress? The importance of recognition. The constructive side of leadership. The do's and don'ts of good supervision.

The substance of communication. Leadership through public speaking. Learning to speak. Prepare better speeches. Really deliver. Create the opportunities to

10. *The Power of Effective Communication* (**Cont.**):

speak. The most powerful tool in the world. Write to communicate. Feed the grapevine. Get the feedback.

Don't let the office trap you. Organize for results. Paper work. The follow-up system. Don't let red tape stop you. Set the priorities. Punch a hole in it. When you are swamped. Let it cool off. Your secretary can double your output. You can't do it all. Be an on-time manager. Activity or accomplishment?

What is the boss looking for? Treat it as your own. Who do you really work for? The kind of politics which pays off. What if you goof? The boss wants results, not problems. Get in good with the boss. Communicate upwards. Get yourself a raise. Disconnect the panic button. Don't be so defensive. Put your boss on the team.

You are on your own. The hazards of playing it safe. Step way out. There is no limit. "If we had." Look for solutions—not scapegoats. What's in it for them? It must be sold.

How managers decide. Decide now; announce later. Write them down. Give it time to hatch. The weighted factor technique. Get the facts. Use your judgment. Don't pass the buck. Nothing can override your own mind. Encourage new thinking. Decisions that make things happen. You can't wait forever. Let your intuition double-check your logic. Delay the impulse. Decide and move on. Select the input. Create them and sell them.

On being promoted. Analyze before you leap. Get
around. Win them over. Watch the pendulum. Don't
be a "therewillbeno". The rules of the game. The mys-
tery of accounting. Let them in on it.

Get to the top. The will to win. Watch the eye level.
Go for 125 percent. Keep it in gear. Plan boldly and
act cautiously. Make it pay. Don't overmanage. There
is lots of room for the individualist. Make sure the meetings help. Pace yourself. Don't play the clown. If it's
concerned with business, it *is* business. Raise the morale.
TFTT in management. Make sure they remember you.

Look beyond the present. The kind of management
tomorrow needs. The age of automation. R & D in
marketing. Changing times. The people side of changes.
The priceless ingredient. R & D in people. Nothing
stays the same. Will you be ready?

For power or performance? The people around you.
The people you pick. The power of your word. Your
stake in the community. Ethics help accomplish business goals. Management is a responsibility, not a goal.

You can't let well enough alone. Your personal curriculum. Mind-stretching. Pull way out in front. A philosophy and a pitch.

1

HITCH YOUR WAGON
TO A STAR

By 1970 this nation will need more than eight million managers or one million five hundred thousand more than there are available today.

There is today and always will be a shortage of top-flight leaders to fill key positions. This book will show you how to become an outstanding executive and how to qualify for one of the many top jobs available today.

Our economy will continue to grow at a rapid rate. The billions of dollars pouring into research and development will produce fantastic new products. Activity will be feverish. Industry will be more complex. So will government, education, and other organized activities.

The need for effective leaders will become more acute. The demand for outstanding people will assure success to those who work for it.

There is and will remain to be plenty of room at the top.

Competition at the top is slim. The man who sets realistic goals and continues to work for them invariably reaches them. There is a great world ahead. The economy will grow and, if you are smart, you will grow with it.

Let us examine some techniques and principles on how *you* can get to the top.

You Can Be Greater Than You Are

You have a price on your head—and the price is exactly what you yourself have set. You are what you think you are (and what you *think,* you are).

Think of the more successful people you know. When they walk into a room it doesn't take long for people to recognize that they are leaders. Why? Because successful people carry the very attitude of success with them. They peg themselves at the top and others assume they belong there.

The way you walk, talk, and act has a lot to do with your success. What *you* think of yourself determines what others will think of you.

If as part of your carriage, demeanor, and attitude you also feel a sincere and genuine interest in others and want them to succeed too, you will go even further. You will assume a true leadership. Your attitude will be one of confidence and not of conceit.

Why Not Now?

To succeed you must have a dream. You've got to fix your eyes on the star you want to reach. You must let your imagination visualize the great heights you want to reach.

There are many people who aspire to greater things. They often put it off, however, and find reasons why they cannot do it now. Or they say, "I'm too old to start now. It's too late."

There was a time when any boy who wore glasses could never hope to play professional baseball. It had never been done and the general belief was that a man just couldn't play baseball if he had to wear glasses. Look at how many professionals wear glasses today. Why? Because a couple of aspiring youngsters wouldn't listen to why they couldn't play. They *wanted* to play baseball. They were looking for ways to get into the game, not reasons why they could not play. They concentrated all of their energy on learning how to play a better game.

If it is worth doing, do it. Forget the obstacles. You'll get by them if you keep your eye on the goal. If it's worth doing, do it *now*. Once you start, the rest is easy.

A trick in getting more done is to write on a slip of paper that which you feel you should do. Don't cross it off until you get it done. It will *nag* you until you get it done.

Getting to the top is worth all the dedication it will take. You will make a lot more. It will give you rewarding opportunities for self-expression and self-fulfillment. It will give you and your family the prestige everyone wants.

If you are success-oriented, if you relish responsibility, if you like to help others, and are basically a happy kind of person, you are halfway to the top.

Let me give you some techniques and suggestions that will assure you of becoming the person you *can* become.

In a Nutshell

There's plenty of room at the top for those who live an attitude of success, fix their sights on lofty goals, and go after those goals with intelligent drive.

2

DEVELOP
WHAT IT TAKES

Getting to the top takes a "can-do" attitude—a positive outlook on life.

It takes a happy sort of person, one who seems to promise satisfaction to those about him. Advertising people have learned long ago that the promise of pleasant experiences sells a lot more merchandise than does the fear of consequences in not having the product.

Success takes characteristics which you have and which you can develop.

Start Something

Success comes to the man who is an innovator, the man who isn't afraid to start something. It is the innovator, not the conformist, who contributes ideas necessary to growth in business.

A man should conform of course to the courtesies of business. He must fit in with the group. He must be a team player.

Above all, however, he must be an individual. The man who parrots others and says what he thinks people want to hear doesn't go very far.

A leader is interested and absorbed in the world about him. He is *alive*.

When you have something to contribute, speak up—not for the sake of hearing yourself talk, but to contribute to the group's progress. Look for new ways to do things. Seek out opportunities. Question everything. Take nothing for granted.

Innovation is the fuel on which organizations feed. No group can grow unless it tries new ideas. The fear of trying anything new, the absence of creative activity, is the cause of failure of many enterprises.

I am not implying that all routines must be upset and the organization be in a constant state of turmoil. Any principle, when carried to extremes, becomes dangerous.

I do mean, however, that you should experiment with some aspects of your job. Be on the lookout for areas that need improvement. Everything good that has ever been tried was pushed by someone with the courage of his convictions. The pessimists will always find reasons why something new should not be tried. Believe it won't work and you would be right. Believe it *will* work, you will again be right—and successful too!

Be Creative

Surround yourself with creative people. Associate with people who have an "anything-can-be-done" attitude. Ask questions. Be sure you know why something is done in a particular way or why it is done at all. Look at all situations from as many viewpoints as possible. Read different kinds of books. Don't let yourself get into a groove on anything you do.

Business can be very exciting. By finding your own particular strengths and talents and building on them, by doing what you believe in and believing what you do, you will reach maximum personal attainment and expression. Success, you will find, is a journey—not a destination. It is a way of life. And it is up to you to create that way of life!

It's the Thought That Counts

Successful people keep an open mind. The *objective* is important, not the way the objective is reached, or whose ideas were followed in reaching it.

Don't be married to preconceived ideas—even if you thought of them yourself. Yesterday's ideas belong to yesterday. The problem today is different. Don't be afraid to have events prove that what you thought last week or last year didn't turn out right. No leader has ever been right all the time. The only man who never makes a mistake is the man who never tries anything.

Beware of the "not-developed-here" concept. Don't resist ideas because they were not thought of or created by you or your group. Accept ideas no matter where they originate. A manager is judged by what he accomplishes, not what he thinks of. If the idea comes from someone else, give him credit but use it if it will help.

Although we use the word "manager" what we say throughout the book is in no way limited to the business world. The principles will apply to the dean of a college, the pastor of a church, the high school principal, the director of a government agency, the dentist, the attorney, or the proprietor running a small business. The principles of successful management apply to all who must get things done.

Of all economic resources, human resources are the least efficiently used. The greatest opportunity for improved economic performance lies in the improvement of the effectiveness of people in their work. Whether any business or other enterprise succeeds depends in the final analysis on its ability to get people to perform.

If At First You Don't Succeed

Asked by an ambitious man for the secret of success, a wealthy business man had this to say:

"You must jump at your opportunity."

"But how can I tell when my opportunity comes?" asked the ambitious youth.

"You can't," replied the business man, *"you've just got to keep jumping."*

Very often when you propose something people will say "Oh, that's been tried before." Worse still, you may find that that is the kind of answer you give to subordinates who come to you with a suggestion or recommendation.

Just because something has been tried before and failed is no reason to assume it will fail again. Chances are the idea was good but the execution and follow through were weak. The timing may have been bad.

If as a result of the previous experience you know some valid reasons why the proposal will not work and those reasons still exist, you wouldn't want to waste time and money again. Turn it down because of specific reasons, but never turn it down merely because "it has been tried before."

If the idea still seems to be good, even though it was tried before, try it again—but see that it is done right this time.

You can't get to the promised land, you know, without going through the wilderness!

Accentuate the Positive

Samuel Johnson once said: "Nothing will ever be attempted if all possible objections must be first overcome." There are two approaches to every opportunity. One emphasizes the things that can be done and the other the obstacles in its path.

Some years ago as a recently appointed Branch Manager, I

found that a number of the salesmen had the habit of meeting at the office before noon and going out to lunch in a group. They would spend an hour or more at the lunch table telling each other how terrible things were. One would start with what a difficult morning he had. The next would tell of the product complaint he was called about, and so on down the line. Each would add to the other's story about what a tough job they had and how impossible things were.

No wonder those men never broke sales records!

I called them together and pointed out what they were doing to each other. I explained and they agreed there were many successes which each man has had, but the atmosphere at the lunch table seemed to call for failure stories.

We broke up the lunch sessions. The lunch meetings were substituted by planned sales meetings at which the successes and the "how-to" were emphasized. The men learned to look at the positive and optimistic side of things.

Their sales and income started to climb almost immediately after they learned to take the positive approach!

Be an optimist. Look for the good in every situation. Look for the opportunities each change presents. You will find the world has more opportunities than problems.

Substitute the word "opportunity" for the word "problem" every time you are tempted to use the word "problem." You will be amazed to see how much more stimulating the word opportunity is. You will find it easier to reach solutions. Your outlook and your thinking will change dramatically when you learn to look for opportunities rather than problems. You will take more positive action. Look at each situation positively and creatively and you will find almost all situations full of opportunities for gain and growth.

Dare to cherish a dream. Dare to *know* it can be done and to know that you are the man to do it. Look for the positive side,

have faith, and you will find that the faith and confidence will
help you to laugh at and *do* the impossible.

The Kind of Breaks You Need

"All you need to succeed are the right breaks. It's all a matter
of luck. It's a question of how the ball bounces."

You've heard these many times: "So and so made it because
he got the right breaks. He was just lucky."

You do need the breaks to succeed, but the kind of breaks
you need are the kind you make for yourself. Let us look into
what goes into making the breaks that assure success. Let us
analyze the kind of breaks you need:

B   in the word "Breaks" stands for *Boldness*. To succeed you
must take risks. You must believe in what you say and
what you do. You must have the confidence and strength
to take bold action. Nothing great has ever been accomplished
without someone risking his time, his fortune, or his future
against great odds.

R   stands for *Reliability*. A successful man is one you could
rely on. He always follows through. He gets things done.
He is a man who finds ways to accomplish whatever he
promised to do. He does not sap his strength or dilute his efforts
looking for reasons why something could not be done.

E   is for *Enthusiasm*. A successful man is *alive*. He is interested in the world about him. He has his eye on the goal
and is persistently driving toward that goal. He never gives
up. He has an undying yearning and inner need to succeed.

A   stands for *Accentuating the Positive*. Success insists on a
"can-do" attitude. It demands optimism. (Have you ever
heard of a pessimist succeeding in anything worthwhile?)
A successful man is cheerful. He has a ready smile and is a pleasure to be with.

K   is for all-important *Knowledge*. A successful man knows
his job. He knows his business. He is not afraid to ask

questions. A successful man has an insatiable thirst for knowledge and drive to do better. He is always learning. Each year he knows more than he did the year before and is a better man than he used to be.

S   stands for *Sincerity*. A successful man is honest with him-
        self. He faces facts as they are, without wishful thinking.
        A man needs the help of many others on his way to the
top. To get their help he must be honest with them. People are not stupid. They see through the most elaborate efforts to fool them. A successful man has a sincere interest in others and a sincere desire to accomplish more.

Yes, you must have the right breaks to succeed. You must be Bold, Reliable, and Enthusiastic. You must Accentuate the Positive, be Knowledgeable, and genuinely Sincere.

These are the kinds of breaks that Beethoven had when he composed such beautiful music even though he was deaf; the kind of breaks Helen Keller had when she accomplished so much even though she was blind and deaf; and the kind of breaks Franklin D. Roosevelt had when he led his nation through most difficult times even though he was stricken with paralysis.

These people didn't complain about getting the right breaks. They made their own.

You will never meet a man who got all the right breaks who didn't have the attributes described above.

If a man blames the breaks he hasn't got what it takes. Things won't always work out as you hoped but it is you and you alone that will determine where you go. When the obstacles pop up, don't let them stop you. Forge ahead that much harder. When things go your way take advantage of them to move even faster than you had planned.

It's Smarter to Give

Here is a secret that will help your income to grow and grow. Work as if you are getting twice as much as you really are. As your income increases, continue to work that way. Stay ahead of the game. Your income will continue to climb with your accomplishments.

The man who says "this is all I am paid to do" is as good as finished. He will never make more. The one who is looking for something for nothing but is afraid to give something for nothing won't make it. He has the whole idea backwards. It works the other way.

If you are making $7,000 a year consider what you would have to know and what you would be expected to accomplish if you were being paid $14,000. Then *learn* what you need to know and *work* to give your employer $14,000 worth of accomplishments.

Before you know it you will be earning $8,000 or $9,000. Don't stop or slow down. Set your sights, goals, and actions immediately to the $16,000 or $18,000 range.

This system works amazingly well.

It works for people in all walks of life. If you are in business for yourself and sell a product for five dollars, give the customer ten dollars' worth. Sincerely try to give him more value. You'll get it back many fold.

The more you give, the more you will get back.

The carpenter who performs like a cabinet maker is never out of work. The messenger who spreads good will for his company while he makes his rounds does not go unrecognized. The clerk who works like an owner finds his income follows his deeds.

The system works, but remember you've got to *give* first, before you receive.

The Secret Source of Energy

What is it that keeps successful men going? Look about you. The people that get so much more done seem to be able to be

on the go all the time. They are never too tired to do what must
be done. They always seem to produce an extra burst of energy
to do a little more.

Where does this energy come from? What is the fuel that
feeds successful people?

The secret is *enjoyment*. Successful people do what they do
because they enjoy it. The work they do is done for its own
sake. You have goals, yes. You work to accomplish them. But
the work itself should be enjoyed!

Work itself—activity—is an achievement. Enjoy every moment
of it. Enjoy what you do. Give yourself to it.

That is the secret of unbounded energy.

3

THE POWER
OF ENTHUSIASM

Enthusiasm can generate the power to drive you to the top. It is the one quality that can be developed and cultivated to the point where it puts you head and shoulders above the crowd.

Enthusiasm is a radiant, vibrant, rejuvenating personal quality which attracts good things, good friends, and good fortune.

Enthusiasm Can Be Cultivated

Enthusiasm can help you to become a star producer, but what if you don't have it to start with? Can it be learned? Can it be cultivated?

It certainly can!

Enthusiasm breeds enthusiasm. It can be developed in many ways. Interest and an insatiable curiosity will develop enthusiasm. The more you learn about your company, your job, and the people you work with, the more excited and enthusiastic you will become. Knowledge, energetically sought after and absorbed, will generate fiery enthusiasm.

Learn in every way you can. Learn from the people you meet. Learn from everything you read. Carry a book with you. Wake up a few minutes earlier each day for extra reading time. Make the most of every opportunity to learn more.

Develop hobbies and interests you can be enthusiastic about. Let enthusiasm become a habit. Enthusiasm developed in your private and social life will spill over into your business life.

Take pride in what you do. Work hard at everything you do. Play hard at your sports. Strive to excel. Hard work is fuel for enthusiasm.

Associate with enthusiastic people, with people who can stimulate you. Seek people with ideas and imagination. Get to know successful people.

Perhaps the most important trick of all is this—even when you don't feel enthusiastic *act* enthusiastic. Enthusiasm is contagious. When you act enthusiastically, those about you will feel the enthusiasm and will catch it. As they become stimulated it will react on you and you will in fact *become* enthusiastic. Such is the power of this wonderful success-building ingredient.

Be Alive

The way to generate enthusiasm in others is to be enthusiastic yourself.

As an executive you will go through feelings of discouragement, loneliness, or just plain gloom, but you can't afford to let that hurt your whole organization. People are quick to pick up a hint of defeat on the part of the boss. Let that attitude get out and all could be lost.

Make sure you keep up *your* morale and your enthusiasm. Get the rest and relaxation you need. Change your pace from time to time. Spend as much time as you can with cheerful, enthusiastic, people. Have wide interests outside of business. It will help you to "recharge your batteries."

Put It in a Positive Frame

To communicate enthusiasm beware of the following pitfalls:

Don't criticize company policies or executives in front of others, unless you could do it where appropriate and in a constructive way.

Praise in public; reprimand in private. Watch your facial expressions and your gestures. See that you do not register disapproval at the wrong time or the wrong place.

Participation Generates Enthusiasm

People who have nothing to say about how things are done are apt to show little interest or concern. They will just drift along on the job, content to get by while doing as little as they can. Involve them in solving problems connected with their jobs and they will join wholeheartedly in finding the solutions.

The method of participation need not always be formalized. It is not always necessary to call a meeting. A manager walking through his department can quite casually and adequately work out solutions with a few of his people at the point of operation. This type of constant informal participation does much to generate enthusiasm in the daily activity.

Radiate Self-Confidence

People will have as much confidence in you as you have in yourself. No more!

You cannot successfully deal with people unless you display a feeling of self-confidence. Nobody wants to be on a ship whose captain doesn't seem to be sure of himself.

Develop and radiate a quiet confidence in yourself. Do that and you will invariably win the confidence of others. Radiate self-confidence. Wear it in a natural manner. There is nothing you cannot do if you put your mind to it. Believe you can, and you will.

Don't feel that you have to make a great show of impressing others with your ability and your responsibility. They know who the boss is. There is no need to parade the fact.

Develop the kind of self-confidence which makes it easier to take criticism. Have enough faith in your ability not to get upset whenever something goes wrong. Everything doesn't always work out just right for *your* boss either.

Don't worry about fancied slights. If someone criticizes, take what could be helpful and ignore what is damaging. Your criticizer is seldom right in everything he says, but he's always got an important point.

If someone else loses his temper, don't feel impelled to lose yours too. Be always in complete control. Look at things in their proper prospective. Find out the whats and whys before making any changes.

Self-confidence can be developed. Learn the job. Study it. *Act* confidently. Apply the techniques discussed in this book. Before long, you will genuinely feel self-confident.

It may help to know that *most* people feel inadequate at times, so don't let an occasional private doubt bother you. When you feel a little unsure, ask yourself, "How would a confident man react in such a situation? How would someone act if he had no feeling of insecurity and if he did not feel as if his position or prestige were being threatened?" Then act just as that confident someone would have acted in your place!

If you are at the top of an organization the self-confidence which you display is important to all members of the group. The way in which the group attacks any problem depends in large part upon the personality and character of its leader. The character of the organization is strongly affected by the character of its chief executive. The self-confidence and enthusiasm of the man on top will be radiated all the way down.

The Quality of Friendship

The kind of guy you are, the sincerity, pleasantness, and optimism which you radiate, will go a long way to getting others to help you move ahead.

People like to be recognized. They want to be liked. They want to be appreciated. Treat everyone as if he were very important in your life (most people *are* that important to you). When you talk to a man, make him feel as if *he* is indeed important. Look at him when you speak. Be aware of what he is thinking and how he is reacting when you speak with him. People will enjoy working with you if they feel you have a sincere interest in *their* needs. They want to do business with people who make them feel important. If they give you a suggestion, make sure you show and *feel* an appreciation for their trying to help you. Think of the outstanding business leaders you know. Do they make others feel important? You can bet they do.

The way to be liked is to like others. Instead of looking for flaws in others look for qualities to admire. Instead of seeking comparisons that seem to favor you, seek matters of mutual interest.

Be appreciative for what is done for you. The waiters in restaurants who say the loudest "thank you's" usually get the largest tips. People like to be appreciated. They will do a lot more for you if you are generous with your thank you's.

When you yourself are praised, don't believe all the good things about you, but don't deny them. Thank them sincerely and graciously, but don't let it go to your head. There are others who don't think you are so great.

Your praises, your thank you's, and your efforts to be friendly must above all be sincere. If you can't say it with sincerity, don't say it at all. Nothing falls flatter than botched attempts at friendship which are obviously sought for selfish gain. If you intend to establish a friendship, make sure you really want to be a friend of the person. It must pass the test "would I want to be his friend if there were no business connection?" If the answer is "no" don't pretend. It won't work.

The way you feel toward others will to a great measure determine the way they will feel about you. People with chips on their shoulders are more likely to find others with chips on their shoulders. This is because we are constantly selecting from experience those aspects which prove our point of view and also because our attitudes toward other people are likely to determine their attitudes toward us. Attitudes of hostility and suspicion tend to provoke similar attitudes from others. Attitudes of friendliness tend to invite attitudes of friendliness in return. Look for the good and the strengths in the other fellow. Offer him sincere friendship. That's the way to build friends.

Consider That Which Will Help You Grow

To be the right kind of leader think always in terms of what can expand your outlook and your environment. Forget the trivial, the negative, and whatever tends to shrink your environment. Pay no attention to the trivial.

Forget your failures. They are past and gone. You can't succeed unless you've tried much more and risked some failures. Don't linger over failures and don't let them hold you back.

Forget your successes too! They too are behind you. Continue to grow and let your subordinates and your associates grow with you.

This is the kind of thinking that will help to make you a better executive.

In a Nutshell

Enthusiasm is the power and fuel which will drive you to the top. It is a power which you can generate within yourself and spread to those around you. Generate it in others by making them truly a part of the team. Develop a self-confidence that will see you through and inspire the others to follow. Recognize people for what they are and what they want to be. Your attitude toward others will decide their attitude toward you.

4

START THE CLIMB

It is never too late to start the climb. Some people stumble along for many years on a mediocre plane and suddenly somehow something happens. It may be unexpected military service, it may be an adversity which the man struggles hard to overcome, it may be the encouraging influence of a smart wife, the reading of an inspiring book, or the meeting of a stimulating person. The reason is not too important.

What *is* important is that many men start the climb later in life. Many people accomplish more in a ten-year span than they do the entire previous thirty or forty years.

Don't ever let yourself think: "If only I had started some years ago. I would have been so far ahead now, but it's too late to start now." I've heard people say, "if only I had gone to college, but it's too late now. . . ." and they will keep saying that for ten years or more. They would have accomplished that goal if they started school the first time they were tempted to say "it's too late now."

Perfection Is a Goal, Not a Path

It's never too late to start. The thrill of accomplishment never diminishes. In one of my classes at night school I had a sixty-four year old man. He worked hard at his studies but he was one of the happiest men I had ever seen. He had always wanted to go to college and he finally got to do it. We all had a great deal of respect for that man who didn't let himself feel "it's too late to start now."

The time to start the climb is simply now—start right now!

The hardest part of any job is to start. You don't know where to begin and you are not sure you will do it right.

If everyone felt this way a single book would not have been written, a musical score composed, nor a new machine designed. An organization would die of inactivity if every project done was not started until the perfect approach was developed.

Do you have to write an important letter but don't know where to start? Just get some thoughts on paper, in any fashion, with any wording. Then work on improving it.

Do you have to prepare a report? Do the same thing.

Do you you have to find a way to sell a new product? Start ringing doorbells. Start asking questions. *Start* the task. You will improve on it as you go along.

Do you want to become a good speaker? Start talking to larger groups. You will get better as you go along.

Do you have to train a group of twenty-five men? Start by training one.

The important thing is to start!

A perfectionist has no place in business. You are working with a dynamic, human, and changing environment. You will never have all the facts you need. The situation will never be perfect.

Your actions and decisions could never be perfect. Make your decisions when you need to. Start your action now. Continue to improve as you go along. Rewrite each chapter over and over again. Rework the musical score as often as you can. Reword the draft of the letter. Improve your selling techniques. Keep working on improvement while you can. "Freeze" on what you are doing *and deliver* when it's more important to *accomplish* than to improve. Work toward improvement, but never insist on perfection.

Work to accomplish goals. Never work for perfection's sake.

Listen to Learn

As an executive you should spend much of your time listening to people. But if you listen and do not hear or do not learn —as so many others do—you will be wasting your time. An executive cannot afford to waste time. There is little of it available and a lot has to be done with what there is.

Most people hear only a fraction of what is said. Many of the things that go wrong do so because someone didn't listen when he should have. A good listener is seldom surprised by later developments. He knows what to expect because he has a feel and understanding of what goes on at the grass roots level. He sees the problem while it is small and before it grows to monstrous proportions. He corrects the small problems and avoids the major disasters.

Poor communications is the cause of most management problems. If you understand what others say, they will understand you and do what you want. Unless you listen, however, and really *hear* you will never understand.

Be careful not to try to "hear" only what you want to. Wishful hearing is bad. Don't fish for statements you would like to hear. Make a sincere effort to really know what people think. If you delude yourself as to the true facts you will soon find yourself face to face with a problem too large to be wished away.

Make notes. You remember only a fraction of what a person has said. You *can't* forget if you make notes.

Taking notes during a conversation can be distracting. You can't maintain eye contact. You can't see the expression on his face, which often tells as much as the words themselves.

Make notes therefore as soon as you can following your conversation, even if it is only to jot down a few key words.

Concentrate while you listen. It is more difficult to concentrate while listening than it is to concentrate while writing or talking. You think faster than the other person talks. While listening, therefore, you continue thinking at high speed while the spoken words arrive at a slower pace. Other thoughts get mixed in while you listen. Your attention is divided between what someone is saying and whatever else you may be thinking of.

Here's what happens. Someone talks to you about a new program which he feels will help the company. You listen but in between you think of other problems. You look at the time. You wonder if the report you prepared has been typed. You come back to the speaker however at frequent intervals and to what he is saying.

You keep up with what he is saying until one of the sidetracks or extraneous thoughts keeps you away from listening a little longer than it should. That report, for instance, was supposed to be typed in double space. Did you tell your secretary or did you forget to?

By the time you get back to your associate you have missed part of what he said. Contact has been broken. You understand less than what has been said.

What can you do about it?

1. Think ahead of the talker. Try to anticipate what he is leading to.
2. Weigh the evidence used by the talker to support what he says. Is he giving the whole story? Is it consistent with what you already know? Does it make sense?
3. Periodically review and summarize what has been said.
4. Put yourself in the speaker's shoes. Establish an empathy with him. What does he feel? What does he want to get done?
5. Listen "between the lines." What is he really trying to say? What are the innuendos? What do his facial expressions, ges-

tures, and tone of voice reveal? Why is he leaving some things unsaid?

6. Keep the speaker on the track. Don't let him stray from the subject. If you let them, many speakers will get into irrelevant sidetracks. Ask questions designed to get him back on the track. Before you guide him back however, make sure he is straying and not really giving you some important background or insight.

Money in the Bank

To zoom ahead you must maintain a sense of independence —a freedom to do what you think is right. You must have the economic ability to stand up for what you feel is right without a panic type of insecurity about your job.

The man without the feeling of security will make panic decisions and will fail.

Build that security. Put a few dollars away each pay day. You've got to spend what you don't save. If you try to do it the other way as most people do—save what you don't spend—you will never make it.

I am not suggesting that you hoard. You *must* increase your standard and way of living as your income goes up. You have to *live* the image you are working to create.

To succeed, however, a man must have the courage of his convictions—and a little money in the bank is vital to that courage.

You Have to Laugh

This might very well be one of the most important suggestions. Learn to see yourself in the right perspective. Don't take yourself too seriously. You will never last the pace if you do. Develop a sense of humor. Life can be funny and you should learn to laugh and relax along the way.

Humor is the ability to see things as others see them. It is the ability to see things in their proper proportions. Some of the most successful executives I know still get a kick out of reading cartoons and funny stories. Try it yourself.

Pick Your Spot

The kind of organization you join will have a lot to do with the kind of success you will enjoy. Is it your type of company? Is the company on the way up? What are the things you should look for?

What kind of person are you? With what kind of people do you like to work? That's the kind of people for whom you should work. To do otherwise is a serious mistake. When the prospective employer is interviewing you, make sure you are finding out what *he* is like at the same time.

Just as different eras and different times require different kinds of leadership (the strong authoritarian did better fifty years ago while the understanding team-player does better today), different companies require different types of leadership.

You will get a lot further if you join the company with whose top management you would feel more in tune. When it comes to picking your company, think Big League. You can't afford to sell yourself short.

You may be better off getting your initial training and experience in a smaller company. It is easier to see the big picture in a small company. This is not an inflexible rule however. Most big companies are really groups of smaller organizations. Each job may involve more people or more money but the task is the same and part of the extra money will often be for you. The important thing is to play in the big leagues. Play where the growth is fastest. That's where the money is.

The advantages of getting an assignment at company headquarters are great. If you do a good job it will be seen and known that much faster. You will be closer to people you can learn from and people who can push you up the ladder.

Before you accept an assignment make sure it is likely to succeed. How well you do often depends on what the elements for success were. No one is likely to remember later the odds you fought against. They will remember only that you did not succeed.

Look for jobs with responsibility. Jobs where you could be counted! Go after the jobs that are the toughest (but where you feel you will succeed). Go for responsibility, not money. Money will follow.

To grow to the top you must be recognized by someone high in the organization. Try to work for people who are moving up. Don't flub the few opportunities you will get to meet the higher ups in the company. Be natural but don't hide.

In picking your spot, analyze yourself and the situation you're in. Are you happy where you are or would you rather be doing something else? Are you taking advantage of your talents and your strengths? How's your company doing? Where is it going? What about your job? Where is it likely to lead? What progress have you made thus far?

Your Wife Is Part of the Team

Management responsibilities will take much of your time and energies. Your wife and family will not see you as often as they might like. It will help a lot if you make your wife part of your team and part of your work.

Keep her informed about what you are doing. Let her participate in evaluations and decisions.

As your position improves, be sure you give her a chance to grow too. Let her meet some of the people with whom you work. If you are getting used to the finer restaurants, take her out to them once in a while also—even if you do it on your own dollar. You must do this to spare possible embarrassment later. Your wife wants to learn as you do to adjust to improving circumstances and changing environment.

Your marriage will be tested against business anxieties, disappointments, success, mortgages, travelling, loneliness, fatigue, and all the pressures of a chaotic modern business life. Make your wife an important part of your business life because if you are success bent, business itself may turn out to be her greatest rival.

What Appears to Be, Becomes

Physical appearance is important to executive success. Clothes could help you to create the image of a leader.

I've known several capable managers who never quite reached the success they were capable of because they didn't have the sense to throw out a shirt that was frayed. They didn't know that a few dollars invested in a successful appearance would have given them the greatest return they ever made on any investment.

A man is often made or broken the moment he puts himself through the doorway. The initial impression will last a long time.

This applies to bearing, speech, and general attitude, as well as to dress. An executive has to look like one. If a hat is the custom, wear one. It won't kill you. Take frequent haircuts. They don't cost that much.

Look like a success if you want to be one. Dream big, act big, and be big. Go first class—you're worth it.

Read for Understanding

You're going to have a lot of reading to do. Knowing how to read will help you to see more, understand more, and do it in less time.

Learn to read faster. Be selective in what you read. Pick out the important things. Scan when appropriate and study when need be. Don't try to be a perfectionist on most of what you read. Read for understanding.

Reading one sentence in a paragraph will often tell you enough. Decide the kind of reading the material calls for: skimming, rapid reading, intensive reading, critical reading, scanning, or a combination of these.

To read faster it is often best to skim quickly through and get to the last sentence as quickly as possible. You could then more carefully reread that which is worth reading more carefully.

Learning to read faster and smarter is a matter of intelligence and push.

Act the Part

On your climb to the top you will be in many different types of positions. You will have to act different types of roles. Gear your thinking and your approach to the job at hand. While you may be qualified for top management you won't get through middle management unless you work well at that level too.

I have seen several cases where the men had outstanding qualities of leadership. People who knew them felt that they may someday be able to fill the top post in the company if they would be able to get through each assignment and through each phase in their management development experience. Many don't make it to the top because they never learn to act the part of the intermediate assignments.

It is important to distinguish the qualities needed by the top executive from those of successful middle-management. Success in one level does not necessarily qualify the man for the top position. There is a big difference between having the technical qualifications for the job and having the outstanding leadership and risk-taking ability of the man at the top. It is the man at the top who really accepts the final responsibility for the big ones and who really sets the course. He is the one who *makes* the policy; most others *interpret* it.

In a Nutshell

1. It's never too late to start. It's earlier than you think.
2. Do the best you can, but get it started.
3. Really listen and you will learn. Read for the purpose of learning.
4. Build some security and deal from a feeling of strength.
5. Learn to relax and laugh at yourself.
6. The company you pick and the job you accept will have ever so much to do with the success you achieve.
7. Make your wife an important and participating part of your team.
8. Look, feel, and act the part you want to project.

5

TO COOK ON ALL BURNERS YOU MUST PLAN ON ALL RANGES

You cannot succeed unless you know where you are going. You must have short range plans, medium range plans, and long range plans. You must know your long term objectives so that your day to day actions could take you toward that goal. Without long term goals much of what you do on a day to day basis could be wasted and would in fact conflict with your own goals. Much of what you do will cancel out other actions on your part.

At the other extreme, unless you have clearly in mind each morning some specific things you want to get done that day you will find that one thing will just lead to the other during the day. You will come home at night "dog tired." You will have been so rushed that you "hardly had time to do anything." You will have accomplished nothing that was important.

Successful people don't do things in spurts. They don't accomplish miracles overnight. They just keep going in the direction they planned to go. They are like the tortoise which keeps inching relentlessly toward the finish line. They *make* it because all of their energies are directed toward clear cut objectives.

They know that success doesn't just happen. They know that success is planned and they work on the plan.

WHAT not HOW

Never discuss means until you have defined the ends.

Most people agree on principles. They agree on what should be accomplished. They will argue, however, for hours on end as to the means of accomplishing those objectives.

Why approach a problem from the difficult point of view therefore when it's so much more effective to think of objectives. Unless you know what you want to see done, there is no point in talking about *how* it should be done.

If you permit yourself to be stopped by artificial obstacles or problems of procedure or administration, you will never succeed in accomplishing anything worthwhile.

Decide on the end to be accomplished. Decide on the "what." Consider the advantages and positive aspects. Decide on the broad concept first, and narrow it down as you go along. Obstacles disappear if you get everyone to think of the ends rather than the means, the *what* rather than the *how*.

What Is the REAL Goal?

Distinguish the important from the trivial. Your ability to do this will have a great bearing on how fast and how far you climb in business.

If it doesn't help to accomplish the long range or medium range goals, forget it. Let somebody else do it.

So much waste motion goes on in business. So much useless information is gathered and transmitted. So many side tracks are followed when you permit someone else to take the initiative on how you will spend one of the most precious commodities you have—time.

Work on that which needs to be done, not because it happens along, but because it will help to accomplish objectives. An executive must be a do-er!

Even the Sky's Not the Limit

One of the ways to accomplish a great deal more is to set visionary and ambitious goals. You will be amazed to see how hard people work to reach the figures that have been set and how creative they can become in developing ways and ideas as to how the lofty goals can be met.

Goals of this kind are set for way in the future. Shorter term goals are set as realistically as possible, but with an eye to reaching the ultimate goal.

Your company or your division may be doing a volume of $500,000. You let it be known that the goal for your group is *ten million dollars* to be reached say in ten years. Once you set that goal everyone, including yourself, will be looking for ways to reach the ten million dollar figure. If you keep at it, you will *reach* the ten million dollars. It may get done in eight years or it might take fifteen, but you will reach it because there are ways to accomplish anything. All you have to do is to find the right ways for you and your company.

Let's take another example of this kind of planning. You may be an assistant accountant department manager at the moment. Set the goal of becoming Vice President and Treasurer in say six years, or even ten years. Everything you do from then on will be directed at reaching that lofty role (keeping alert though to other opportunities that might come along). Keep at it until you have reached it (by which time you will have set a still loftier role) or until you have changed your long-term goal to something else. Many people have reached success by following this technique.

The Basics of Planning

Managers must regularly plan to prepare their organizations for definite needs, probable developments, and uncertain eventualities in the years ahead. Markets, products, the qualifications of people needed to staff the operations, manufacturing methods, and other important factors are changing all the time. The company that triggers a well-planned shift often fares better than the one who follows a "me too" role.

Many significant developments are the result, not of a sudden flash of genius, but of years of persistent yet imaginative scientific, engineering, or other effort. Great numbers of decisions and steps are usually required for product development, for organization changes, for plant construction, for raising new capital or for distribution changes. Needs must be identified and acted on long before the result is required.

Despite the impossibility of accurately forecasting the future, as a business executive you must identify a range of possibilities and prepare for them.

"Forecasting" is the attempt to find the most probable course of events or range of possibilities. "Planning" is deciding what you will do about them.

Specialists in market research and economic forecasting can be useful in gathering information on which plans for the business can be based. Decisions on what is to be achieved, however, are business decisions to be made by responsible managers.

When undertaking a formal planning effort for the first time, two thoughts are suggested:

Don't expect perfect results on the first try.

Set some kind of time limit to getting your plans on paper.

There are always going to be changes. Some managers may

say, "Let's not start planning until we get this piece of information or that set of facts." Get something down to start with even though it will be revised later.

Planning to solve a problem is actually the second step. The first thing that must be done is that the problem must be clearly defined. Planning takes place after the problem has been defined.

Objectives must have realistic purposes. What are the problems? What are we really trying to achieve? What *should* we accomplish?

The decision to reach 200 million dollars in gross sales in five years may not be a proper objective. It may be set as an objective because the chief executive thinks it would be good to achieve. What about profits? Is $200 million an optimum size for this company in five years? What will it cost? What problems will it present? What opportunities will it reveal? Will it fit in with the other objectives set for the company?

In setting objectives, the capabilities of your group must be understood. Realism and insight play an important part here. Is it a manufacturing company with sales facilities? Is it a marketing and engineering company with production plants? In what way is the organization *unique*? How can this uniqueness be taken advantage of?

Objectives should be established because their achievement is essential. It is not always easy to determine what is essential and what is not. Setting goals for yourself and for others requires keen discrimination between the essential and the merely desirable.

The setting of objectives helps to prevent oversights. You should however guard against setting so many goals in unimportant areas that you lose sight of major opportunities.

The elements of objectives should be sparse rather than abundant. No matter how thoroughly you plan, you cannot think of and provide for everything that might happen. As events evolve, it is far better to have in mind the essentials rather than to be encumbered with the trivial.

Considering alternative courses of action helps to provide for the unexpected. A good manager should never be taken by complete surprise. He must never allow important situations to develop without having foreseen their possibility and made some tentative plans. A man who knows his business and who keeps up with what is taking place around him is never really surprised.

Planning Is a Flexible Tool

A plan is not an end in itself. It is a way to reach a desirable goal. A plan is never a finished product. You can never really "freeze" on a plan and say "this is it." Such would be a *wish,* rather than a *plan.*

Plans must remain flexible. You will never have all the facts when you make your plans. You will never be able to see clearly into the future. The plan you devise therefore is the best you can do at the time. It must be alterable. It must be used as a guide—not a hard and fast commitment.

Plans are based on what has happened so far, what is happening now, and what we think will happen in the future. The future, when it comes, is *never* as anticipated and a plan that cannot be changed as conditions change is worse than no plan at all.

Plans should be realistic as well as relevant to objectives and environment. The plan is the link between the present and the future. The link must not be broken. Plans should not be based on wishful thinking but should be built on a solid foundation. Any plan should consist of several smaller plans so that parts can be speeded up, slowed down, or changed.

Anticipate the Unexpected

Complete planning is impossible.

Where possible alternatives should be developed for whatever may come up. You cannot afford to be caught by surprise, by something you never even thought might happen and for which you have no plan at all.

Planning, whether the formal kind for your company, or the personal kind for yourself, must be done on a regular and continuing basis. It should be a continuing process.

No one can foresee the entire future. You must continue to check on how the plan is working so that problems can be recognized and dealt with promptly.

It Must Be Customer Oriented

What about the people who are paying the bills? What do the *customers* want?

This in the long run should do much to shape the course of management decisions and executive actions—what will the ultimate bosses want?

We live in a consumer dominated economy. The consumer decides what shall be made and who shall make it. By his vote in the market place, the customer designates which corporations shall survive and which shall perish. The *consumer* is the real Head of Research or Director of Marketing.

Keep your mind on that consumer when you make your business plans. He won't buy unless it is what he wants. If he doesn't buy it you will be out of business. It's as simple as all that.

Everything in a business, every department, must be influenced by what the customer will buy and how to get it to him at a profit. Every function within the company must be geared to accomplishing that goal and the connection should be as direct and as close as possible.

Keep this in mind and your business decisions will be right so much more often. Plan with the customer in mind.

No Growth Without Profits

There are two major forms of economic systems in the world today—communism and the private enterprise profit system.

Profits provide a powerful and effective motivation for people to produce. The profit system has created more jobs and has given people more comforts than any other system ever has at any time in history.

The profit system is one we should be proud of and one which we must fight to protect and improve for the benefit of all.

There are many objectives in business, but a basic one is and must remain the creation of adequate profits. No business can grow or long exist without it.

Your planning and your executive action must always keep in mind that you are in business to make a profit and that you need a profit to stay in business.

Some of the misguided attitudes about profits reminds me of a story which made the rounds a few years ago. A man applying for a new job asked the interviewer:

"Does your company guarantee any overtime?"

"No," he was told, "you work as required and get paid for what you do."

"Last place I worked they paid overtime every week, whether you worked extra or not."

"Then why did you leave?"

"The company folded up."

Precheck the Moves

Forecasting and budgeting are essential tools of management.

A budget is a plan and a standard. Budgeting helps to set realistic goals and guides you to the achievement of those goals. Budgeting is an instrument of control and a tool for a more effective job. It can help you to keep your eye on your goals and to direct your efforts into more productive channels.

By forecasting and budgeting into the future you can see the probable results of alternate courses of action. Increased sales at an increasing cost might show that in five years a smaller profit will be produced than if the sales growth were slowed down and costs kept low. Or you might find that with a relatively fixed overhead over the next few years *adding* more salesmen and increasing selling and advertising costs could materially *increase* profits over a few years span.

Good forecasting enables you to work these alternatives out on paper before a lot of time and money is wasted—and prevents you from making some serious mistakes that could have been avoided by good budgeting.

Budgets should be set realistically. Don't underbudget by setting targets that are easy to beat or overbudget by setting targets that are unattainable. If you underbudget your superiors will feel your sights are too low and will wonder if they have the right man in the job. If you overbudget and fall short of the mark they will again wonder if you are the man for the job.

Budgets should be flexible and should allow for changes in business conditions. The short term forecast and budget should be specific while the long term forecast and budget is set up on broader terms. Long term budgets represent the direction to which all efforts are placed. Make the long term goals as ambitious as you dare. Make sure everyone in your organization knows what the objectives are. Everyone must have a goal to shoot for and a guide for carrying out his activities.

In a Nutshell

For more effective day to day actions keep your eye on realistic long range goals. The end or goal is much more important than the means or procedure followed in reaching your goals. Set priorities and work on the essentials. Dare to set sights that are far reaching, bold, and ambitious. Changes will come but will benefit only those who plan for them—only those who create the changes.

Needs must be identified and acted upon long before the result is required. Learn to take advantage of unique strengths in yourself and your company. Planning is a continuous process which changes the future and is changed by the future. Planning provides for the unexpected and, above all, is customer oriented. It recognizes the need to produce a profit as a real measure of economic and business progress and a source of funds for business and social progress. Budgeting helps to determine what results are likely from specific courses of action. It enables you to re-plan before you consume costly time or dollars.

To really accomplish, you've got to have plans.

6

YOU CAN'T DO IT ALONE

No matter how fast you work or how smart you work you will accomplish little unless you can get others to help you. The more people you can get who can get more done, the higher you will rise.

Attracting, recruiting, selecting, and managing people is an important function of a good leader. Some of the brightest men, many of whom were absolutely brilliant, have failed as executives because they never learned to work through people. The inability to judge and motivate people will absolutely bar a man from reaching or holding a top management job.

Get the Right People

A top man for one company could be a problem for another. A good qualification for one job could be an obstacle for another. Before you even start to look for people you need to ask: What kind of company are we? What are our unique strengths? What are we trying to accomplish? What qualities do we need most? What type of experience is likely to best fit the rest of the group?

Before you recruit for a specific job you've got to narrow down your questions still further. What kind of person could best fill the spot? Should he be creative? Do we prefer a thorough organizer? Should he be outgoing? Must he be especially careful about details?

Before *you* can move ahead you will need to bring in and develop people who could assume more tasks from you. Your ability to bring in the right people and to develop them will to a major degree determine whether you will move up, stay where you are, or move out.

A company needs all kinds of managers for different levels of jobs.

Some jobs require people with heavy technical skills. In filling these jobs make sure you get the most proficient engineer, accountant, salesman, or other specialized man. Most people who move into management start at this stage. To do well at it you must become an expert. You must learn all you can and be as proficient as possible in your specialty. This is the stage at which you say "I will be the *best* inventory clerk, the best salesman, or the best accountant in the business."

If you want to be an executive, however, remember that this is only the start and a stage you should move *through*. You will move up faster if you do the first job well, but you will never move up if you do not at the proper time learn and demonstrate your knowledge and ability in broader areas.

So in hiring at the technical stage you must ask "what has the man done and what can the man do?" The best indicator of what a man will accomplish in the future is what he has accomplished in the past.

This is true no matter how young the man may be. If he just got out of school, what were his grades, how did he get along with fellow students and teachers, in what extra activities and service assignments did he participate? What odds did he work against? Did he carry a heavy program? Did he have to work all or part of his way through? All of this helps you to judge the total man.

If he is older his work and social history will tell you a lot about how well he will do in the future.

Most jobs require the ability of the man to work effectively as a group member and to build cooperative effort within the team he leads. Some jobs require this more than others. Middle management jobs probably require this ability most of all.

Again, as far as you are concerned, if you want to move up from the technical or specialized stage, you *must* perfect your human skills.

The higher the job, the greater the need for people who can see the broad picture, people who know the important from the unimportant, people who have the right perspective. Decisions become more important. They affect more people and more dollars. The top man can't afford to be wrong on the big decisions. Too much rides on it.

Know Where to Look

You cannot wait until the vacancy is created before you start to look for the person to fill it. You certainly can't do this for key spots.

Recruiting is a continuing process. Good managers are always on the lookout for top people. The ideal situation is to know people who are employed elsewhere but who are capable and available should you want them. When a vacancy occurs you need but to call them. You never reach this ideal in all situations, but you work toward it.

Don't wait for people to come to you. Recruiting is an *active* process. The right people seldom come on their own. You *look* for them. You seek them out, and you *sell* them on making the change.

Your future depends on the people you get. You can't entrust your future to chance.

There are many sources for new employees. I will list a few

but the total list includes all that your imagination, ingenuity, and persistency can lead to:

1. *Advertising.* Some newspapers are better than others. Find out which they are. What kind of results have others had in your city? Special advertising agencies will help you to select the paper, write the ad, and will place the ad at no extra cost to you. They receive a commission from the newspaper. The newspaper charges you the same price whether you place your ad direct or through an agency.

2. *Employment Agencies.* There are all kinds of agencies—some very good and many mediocre or worse. Most of them work on commissions. The more people they place the more money they make. The more people they get you to see the more likely you are to hire one of them. If you let them get away with it, many will do no screening at all. They will send you lots of anybodies and waste your time.

   Here too, seek out the good agencies. Through trial and through asking, find the one or two who can do the best job in finding the kind of people you need. Visit them or let them visit you. Tell them something about your business and your company. Use them as employment consultants. Without tying yourself to an exclusive arrangement, make it worth their efforts by indicating your intent to work closely with them. Tell them what other sources you are using. If you are not using many, if they know they have a good chance of placing the right man, they will do a lot of the work for you. They will advertise and they will seek the man out.

   In order to avoid seeing many applicants who are not even close to what you are looking for you might follow the rule of never seeing a man referred by an agency unless you first see his résumé. Seeing the wrong applicants can tie you up in knots and prevent you from accomplishing your important tasks.

3. *Personal Contact.* This is often the source for the best people you will find. The more seeking out you personally do, the better people you will hire. Friends and business associates can

help. Industry and professional association meetings will give you the opportunity to meet and evaluate potential employees.

4. *Your Personnel Department.* If your company has one, use it. They could help you to find the people you want. Be candid with them. If practical, tell them what you need and who you are working with. Use them too as your recruiting consultants. Don't stop there. Your job is to get the best people. Be sure you pick the one *you* want. No well run company will expect that the personnel department's judgment will supersede that of the man who has the responsibility for accomplishment.

Interview for Results

Perhaps the best advice I could give you on interviewing is "don't talk too much." This is curiously true whether you are the applicant or the interviewer. If you want to learn what the other fellow is like, you've got an awful lot of listening to do.

Make him feel at ease when he comes in—really make him feel at ease. Make sure there is eye contact. Establish some kind of feeling or rapport. This could be done in just a few moments if you are sincere about wanting to do it and are sympathetic with the applicant's feeling. Rapport is established by the friendly, considerate attitude of the interviewer, not by chit-chat.

Outside of that, however, let *him* talk. If you talk more than half of the time, you are not interviewing. You are being interviewed.

What is he looking for? What does he think is important? What is his attitude and outlook? How will he fit in? These are the questions you ask yourself while he talks?

Ask questions that require more than a yes or no answer. To get truthful answers about preferences, make alternate answers appear equally acceptable. Give him time to think and time to answer. Give him time to elaborate. A few moments of silence intelligently dispersed will help to accomplish this.

If he is obviously not the kind of man you want, get rid of him. Nicely, of course, but direct the remaining moments to letting him down politely, feelingly, and sympathetically. Let him down and let him out.

If he is the kind of man you want, start to narrow the conversation just a bit. Tell him something of the company or give him something to read at home. Be accurate in whatever you say. Don't exaggerate and don't oversell. Describe the job enough to build up interest but don't go into too much detail until a later interview.

If the man is important enough for you to make the selection, it is important for you that the right choice be made. See an applicant more than once. Employment decisions should never be made after one interview. See him again at least a few days later. Many applicants who look good at the first interview fall down measurably at a subsequent meeting. They may be off guard the second time and their true self is more likely to come through. You would have had a chance to think of some of the areas you want to question him on more deeply and it may show some serious flaws.

You may have talked to some of the people he worked with and perhaps are looking for specific factors the next time you see him.

As basic as it may seem, a poor job is often done in checking references. Professional organizations such as the Retail Credit Company can do a good checking job for you. The fee is nominal and they should be used.

You however must personally check some references if the man is to work for you. I don't normally bother with the personal references the applicant lists. Obviously they will give him a good reference or he wouldn't have given their names.

Check the people he worked for and the people he worked with. The person he listed on the application blank may not be the best one to talk with. One or two calls will get you to the man best able to give you a meaningful story of what the man has done, what he can do, what his strengths are, and what his shortcomings are. If two or more people mention a specific weakness and if that would be detrimental in the job, probe that point as far as you can.

In asking for information, don't put words in the other person's mouth. Too often people ask the question, and before the other fellow has gotten three words out in reply, the asker will say "I'm glad to hear that. We were very impressed with Mr. Applicant and believe he could do a good job for us. I'm glad you found him to be very satisfactory." Give the man a chance to tell you what he *really* thinks. It's very important to you.

Checking references by letter is not very satisfactory. You will never get to know your candidate that way. You will merely verify some data. You must feel you really know the man before you hire him.

Unsolicited letters of reference from previous employers mean nothing. A cartoon which recently appeared in the *Wall Street Journal* illustrates this. It showed the boss talking to a rather dejected looking character and the caption read: "If I give you good references, will you consider working for one of our competitors?"

Take notes during the interview if you can comfortably and naturally do so. Make them as brief as possible—just a word or two here and there will often do. You can fill in the details after he leaves. Don't make this an investigation or an inquisition. Keep the contact and maintain an atmosphere which encourages him to relax and talk.

Ask yourself throughout the interview, *can* he do the job and *will* he do the job?

Tests Are Tools, Not Crutches

Some excellent tests are available. There are a number of reliable industrial psychological firms. Properly used these, like all other tools of management, could help you. Improperly used they could hurt you and the candidates.

Make sure you are using appropriate tests. Don't test for word intelligence when you need conceptual skills. Make sure the psychologist knows your company, knows the people the applicant will be working with, and knows the type of job the applicant is being considered for. Remember always that *you* must make the decision. These tools are designed to help you. But *you* must decide! You could conceivably hire a man who shows up poorly on a specific test or pass up a man who is recommended by the psychologist. The decision is yours to make. The state of the art is still such that human judgment must be exercised. There is no exactness where people are concerned.

If a test, or an interview, or a reference check indicates a possible weakness or failing, however, don't ignore it. Your job is to determine if the test or the check was right. If a test, for instance, shows a man to be low in intelligence, you stop and consider. Did the man seem dull? Probe into this at the next interview. What do his references say about his intelligence? What kind of grades did he get in school? The amount of checking you do will depend on your conviction as to whether the test was right or wrong in this respect. If when you are through you decide the man has the necessary intelligence and that the test was wrong, that's it. Don't be bound by the one test.

If the psychologist feels he may be short on organizational ability or attention to details and this is significant to the job, reflect a moment. If it seems to fit in with what you have seen so far, that's it. You don't want the man. If it doesn't seem to fit in, probe and investigate until you convince yourself one way or the other.

If everything seems to point the wrong way—the tests, the psychologist, and the credit references—you don't hire him. If despite the negative reports you still like him he is probably reminding you of someone else who looked like him but who had better qualities.

Look at the Entire Man

Before you hire him, know him well. The interview, the tests, and the credit checks are designed to help you. Does it all fit together? Does he make sense for you? Are the past ten or twelve years of his life completely accounted for? Will you be able to work with him? What about his employment record? Has he had many jobs in the past few years? This might be all right for a younger man just starting out, but may not be good for the mature applicant.

Speaking of maturity, if you are interviewing a young candidate for a job that will grow in responsibility, he has to have the basic qualities right then and there. Good leaders mature early. If he is not grown up enough or responsible enough by the time he is being considered for the job, chances are he never will be.

You could tell pretty early in life if a boy is going to be successful. What he has done before is a pretty good barometer of what he will do in the future.

By his late teens or early twenties the future executive is often increasingly interested in the type of work or profession he will follow. He develops a willingness to work, study, and sacrifice for the sake of a long-range career.

As he grows up he is work-centered in the broad sense of trying to build a business, a career, and a way of life that is economically, socially, and spiritually satisfactory. He measures his success by his worth and service to others and by his self-development, rather than just by money and power.

The Spots Don't Change

Be extremely critical when hiring people. If the man was sloppy before, don't assume he will change. If he was overbearing to his subordinates in the past, assume he will be so in the future. If he made several real bad errors in judgment, let him go by. When it comes to hiring a man, assume the leopard never changes his spots.

Be as inflexible as can be in hiring a man. He's got to measure up to your high standards.

Once you have him, though, no matter who originally employed him, and no matter what problems he may have, be as sympathetic and helpful as you can be. Bring him along and build him up if you possibly can.

It is generally well for the man who is going to be the applicant's immediate boss to make the selection and the hiring decision with the approval of the next immediate superior. Having two people cooperate on the selection makes it possible to discuss the applicant between the two who are most anxious that the man be a good employee. It further is good sense to have your boss pass on your immediate subordinates because they will be helping you to accomplish some of the goals which your boss has helped to set.

Pick the Stars

The standards you set for the people you hire will have a lot to do with the quality of your organization. Look for the people who have demonstrated outstanding ability. Try to get the future star early in his career while you could still afford him and while you could train him according to your company's needs. Look for the man with the higher potential.

Don't be one of those people who consciously or unknowingly try to steer away from a man who might be too good. They actually look for mediocrity. If you think you shouldn't hire a man who might turn out to be better than you, you shouldn't be reading this book because you won't become a top executive anyway. If you are more concerned with what looks like security than with opportunity, the ceiling for you will be very low indeed.

The man who surrounds himself with mediocrity is often more secure for a while but he is really running the greater risks in the long run. He won't be pushed out for some time. What will happen, however, is that his group will accomplish less and less. His superiors will not promote a manager like this and may in fact eventually fire him. The risk of taking the seemingly safer path of hiring mediocrity is indeed the greatest risk you could assume.

By hiring the stars you impose upon yourself the need to keep growing and keep improving. The better subordinates *will* push you out of your job, but they will be pushing you *up* into the higher position. You've got to assume risks anyway. Why not assume the kind that is likely to give you greater rewards?

There are many diamonds in the rough—people who have not had the advantage of good supervision, good environment, or good training. There are many who are hungry for success and accomplishment, who are yearning to get ahead. Find those people. Give them the guidance and stimulation they need, and you will have developed some outstanding associates.

Look for people with basic qualities. Does he have imagination, initiative, ingenuity, and *above all* integrity? Is he honest with himself? Does he face the facts? Does he have a sense of proportion? If the man has these qualities and is sufficiently intelligent he will learn the details of the job. This is the man you should look for rather than the one with the specific experience, but poor personal qualities.

I've made it a practice not to hire personal friends or relatives. It's not fair to everyone concerned, including the other people that are working for you. I look at it this way. If the man is that good he'll be able to make it on his own. He won't need your personal guardianship. He'll go a lot further on his

own without the artificial pressures of your personal relationship. (Help him to get a job in another department or another
company, if you wish, but don't have him work for you.) If
he's not that good, you can't afford to have him either.

In looking for the stars, be careful not to narrow the field
unnecessarily. Don't let preconceptions eliminate the ones who
could accomplish more. Keep an open mind till you think you
know the man and judge him for what he is, what he can do,
and what he will do.

Some good recruiters, incidentally, won't hire a man unless
the applicant calls *them* after the interview. They prefer to see
some enthusiasm and initiative on the part of the candidate.
You might want to try this technique too.

Make It Worthwhile

Establish a reputation for being fair and for helping people
to grow and your recruiting will be made much easier. You will
attract more and more of the kind of people you will need to
help you in your executive growth.

Many managers still live by the concept that no employee
should make more than his boss. This is wrong. This sometimes
puts a lopsided value on management versus some special skills
more directly productive of corporate growth.

Were it not for the skill of the individual producers there
would be no bosses. Top salesmen often make more than their
sales managers, and rightly so. They often *contribute* more.

A good baseball manager is happy to have outstanding stars
on his team who make more money than he does. One is a good
manager and is paid as such. The other is a star performer and
is paid as such. The amount of money each makes has nothing
to do with the fact that the manager calls the signals and the
player follows them.

Having the best men you could get and paying them what

they are worth will assure you of greater accomplishment.

Pay your people more. You will be able to demand more in return.

Once you get them, however, don't rely entirely on good pay, fringe benefits, and pleasant working conditions to motivate your people to do better. These are the things which will influence people in wanting to join your company, but they cannot be regarded as incentives.

These are the types of conditions which help to fill the psychological and more basic needs of people. Once fulfilled, however, they are not motivators. Food is not an incentive after you've had a good meal. Pleasant surroundings are not an incentive to do more if that is what you have been used to. Insurance coverage is not an incentive for you to do better when you already have a sense of security. These things motivate people only when they don't have them.

The way to motivate your people is to make them a part—a real part—of what is being done.

You Might Already Have Him

In more times than not the man you need is already working for your company. Make it your business to know the people down the line. See if you could pick out the winners among them. Promote them when you can.

Promotion must be based on proven performance. If he's the man for the greater responsibility, move him up. Nothing does more harm than the refusal to promote a good man because he is too important in his present job.

Make full utilization of *all* people who work for you. The situation in which promotions go only to salesmen, or engineers, or accountants, is destructive of the group which is by-passed and is a terrible waste of scarce and expensive talent.

In a Nutshell

You can't do it alone. Get the best qualified people for the jobs that have to be done. Help new employees to adjust to the job and to the group. Provide opportunity for people to improve their skills and abilities. Evaluate performance of people on a systematic and fair basis. Create in your people a desire to do an even better job. Keep informed on how each person is doing. Move the best people up the promotion ladder. Get the right people. Help them grow. That's the way for you too to continue to grow!

7

MANAGEMENT BY GEORGE [1]

Here in a few words is a management philosophy
that will help to make you a great leader:
Let George do it.
He wants to.
All you have to do is tell him what needs to be accomplished
and why, and possibly show him how.

You will accomplish a lot more if you create an environment
whereby others are encouraged to do more, to take more responsibility, and to learn more.

By helping others to grow, you and your organization will
function more efficiently, profits will go up, people will be
busier, and happier too.

That's the simple philosophy behind delegation—the type of
delegation that shows real confidence in your associates and a
sincere desire to help them grow.

Yes, let George do it. He could often do it better than you
can if you give him the facts, the confidence, and the encour-
agement.

The trick simply is to:

1. *Determine what really needs to be done.* A large amount

1 "Management By George," by the author, originally appeared in *Sales Management,* October 19, 1962.

of current activity may not be necessary at all. "Busywork" and habits have a way of creeping into the daily routine. Eliminate that which does not help to meet objectives.

2. *Find the George who can do it.* He may be in your organization now or available through good recruiting. There are many Georges who can do the job if you recruit aggressively, select carefully, train properly, and let them do the job.

3. *Train him to do it.* Give him all the background and reasons why. Let him accomplish the task in his own way. There might be a better approach than the one you were thinking of.

4. *Let him do the job!* With tasks and objectives well defined and people properly selected and trained, you can accomplish a lot more by letting George do it.

He will grow and, by George, you will too! [2]

---

[2] Here in a few words is the very essence and core of good management. More detailed suggestions on how to make this management philosophy work for you will be found within the other chapters of this book.

8

IT'S THE SCORE
THAT COUNTS

Delegate by goals and accomplishments. State what you want done rather than *how* you want it done. Set the task in broad terms. Let the man who is going to do the job determine the best way to reach the goals.

Without clearly defined goals and clear-cut assignment of responsibilities, many will be performing day to day tasks which tend to lead the company in different directions. By using good organization and management practices people will accomplish company goals in shorter time and with less activity or effort.

Your people must know exactly what is expected. If they know they will be judged by accomplishment of specific objectives they will work harder to accomplish those objectives. You will be amazed to see how much more you can get done.

You should be able to write down in clear concise language what you expect of each subordinate. If you can't write it down, don't expect it to be done.

Delegation gets the job done and develops a group capable of doing even more in the future. It helps to develop leaders all the way down the line. People grow when you give them responsibility and opportunities to make decisions.

It is very difficult sometimes to watch a subordinate make a mistake, especially when you know he is going to make it. People learn most from their mistakes, yet you don't want the man to make a serious error.

A good rule is to let him make small mistakes but stop him from making the big ones.

When you stop him, give him all the background you can to explain why the proposed action would have been wrong. Let him learn from the mistakes he does not make as well as from the ones he makes.

If you find yourself loaded with details or if you find that too many things that could be handled by others are being referred to you, chances are you have not clearly organized and delegated. If your door is "always open" to the extent it is jammed with subordinates waiting for instructions, your business survival may depend on your learning to delegate.

Don't Abdicate

Be careful, though. You can overdelegate. If the door is always closed, nobody comes in, and you never seem to be faced with the need to make a decision, you are in even worse trouble. You may have overdelegated to the point of abdication.

No business could long survive if the man at the head abdicates, leaving no one else in full charge. Get out and see what is going on. If your responsibility includes a department covering an entire floor, get around that floor. If your responsibility takes in a continent, get around that continent to see for yourself. Travel is more and more a way of business life. You've got to delegate the responsibility, but you must make sure the job is getting done.

Don't regret later that you "gave him more rope" than you should have. Delegate, but don't abdicate.

Lighten the Load for Higher Flight

The kind of delegation we are talking about is the kind that encourages participation by you and your subordinates in mutual problems and the kind that puts responsibility where it could result in the greatest accomplishments.

Remember this. The real source of authority possessed by a manager lies in the *acceptance* of its exercise by those who are subject to it. It is the *subordinates* who determine the authority which a manager may use. Formal authority becomes real authority only when it is accepted.

Why does one youngster stand out in a group? Why do the rest look to the one to determine what the rules of the game will be, who will play first base, and who will bat fourth? What kind of authority does that one boy have? *He has the kind of authority that results from acceptance by others to his leadership.* It is the group which gives him his authority and it gives it to him because of the leadership characteristics which he displays.

Delegation is one sure way of preparing yourself for further climb up the executive ladder. Delegate all you can. As soon as you know a task well and have set it down to a routine or have established a policy governing it, delegate the task. Leave yourself time to learn other tasks and to prepare yourself for the job ahead.

Never do what you can delegate. Never do what someone else can do better.

If you spend most of your time with the same subordinates you may be trying to run their jobs for them. Do you call them in every time you think of something or do you save it for your next meeting?

Are actions often held up waiting for your personal approval or instructions? Do you find yourself making the same *type* of decisions over and over again? Let your subordinates make them. Better still, *insist* that they make them.

Here's something you could try. Every night write down something you did that day that you will never have to do again because you have trained someone else to do it. There's real power in this one.

Keep yourself free to check whatever *you* want to look at and whenever you want to do so. Let others do the routine checking.

You will achieve a higher degree of success when you learn to delegate and learn to use participative forms of direction. You've got to be sincere about it however. Don't try to encourage participation and the acceptance of responsibility unless you *really* want to know what the others think and really want to make use of the opinions and ideas of the people on your team. A manager who uses this kind of management as a clever gimmick is quickly labeled by the group for what he is—a plain ordinary phony.

"Management by George" is based on genuine respect for the individual. It goes hand in hand with the belief that all men are endowed with intelligence, free will, and the responsibility to think for themselves. This kind of management can unleash productive forces with explosive potential power and impact.

You Are Not a Switchboard or the Neck of a Bottle

Don't insist on rigid communication channels. Don't insist that everything go through you or that you get a copy of everything. Leave it up to them and hold them accountable for letting you know what you should know and asking your approval when it is necessary and proper to do so.

If a matter could be handled by having people cross organiza-

tional lines, let them. Organization charts are supposed to help
in management, not to interfere with accomplishments. As long
as they keep you posted on important developments encourage
them to go to the one who could help the most.

Refer your subordinates and your superiors directly to others
in your organization who can answer specific questions better
than you can. You're not supposed to have every bit of information at your fingertips. You're supposed to see that things get
done. You're supposed to encourage enthusiastic and intelligent action on the part of all people in your organization.
You're *not* supposed to be a bottleneck or a message center.

Stay on Top of the Job

Everyone has his own style of management. Never try to be
anyone but yourself.

Constantly reappraise how much you can delegate to each
man. Some could handle more. They are the ones who will
move ahead. Others get swamped from the word go.

To assure your own growth you must be able to accept more
and more while you train others to delegate much of what you
accept. Your job is to get it done. Nobody cares whether you do
it yourself—just as long as it gets done. Just as long as you are
the one to go to when a job needs to be done.

A perfectionist cannot rise in business. It may not be done
as well as you would have done it yourself, but if you try to do
too much yourself, it won't be done at all. The more you try
to do yourself, the more you will *have* to do yourself. Your subordinates will never learn how.

Don't be afraid your people will learn to do some things
better than you can. They are *supposed* to do it better. They
are supposed to know more about the specifics of the job. Your
job is to get the task *done*. You will get paid a lot more for

knowing how to get it done than for knowing how to do it.

Many refuse to delegate because of a sense of insecurity. They are afraid someone may learn to do their job as well or better. If that is what you want, all right. Don't let anyone know what you are doing. You will have security that way—security from moving ahead. You will be given fewer and fewer important jobs and you will end up at the bottom of the heap.

If you keep learning, however, continue to become more valuable, and free yourself for better assignments by delegating, you will earn far greater security—the kind of security that comes from growth. You will always be worth a lot more.

Assure the Payoff

Getting the right people and passing a share of the load to them is only a small part of what needs to be done. To assure the payoff your people have to be well trained, well directed, and adequately helped.

Develop a reputation for building people and you will attract better men and women to come to work for you. Here are several points to keep in mind in developing subordinates:

1. *Find the Time.*

You must do some personal coaching for those who report to you. Tell them what you expect them to know and what you want them to do. Tell them how they could improve themselves. Stimulate them to learn more. Pass along or suggest some reading material. Everyone who works for you should benefit from his association with you. If he doesn't you have wasted part of his most productive period.

2. *Be Tolerant of Mistakes.*

If you are a boss, chances are that you have made a few mistakes yourself before you got to where you are. That is something you should never forget.

If the man learns from his mistakes, fine. If the mistake was made because he was trying to do something new and not because he is stupid, again fine. People learn from mistakes, and you do want them to learn.

The risk that led to a mistake is often the type that leads to innovations and improvements. The only man who never makes a mistake is the one who never tries something new.

People learn from their own experience. What we can do most effectively is to help them in this process. *You* cannot change them. You must give them an opportunity to change themselves, if they wish, by reflecting upon and re-evaluating their own experience. Don't try to change them, but do try to help them change.

3. *Be Considerate.*

Be sure you know the man. As his boss you are one of the most important people in his life. He looks to you for guidance and for approval. The tone you set will help determine how happy he will be at his work, and no one performs well unless he likes what he is doing. Your employees can make unlimited contributions if given the opportunity.

4. *Let Him Be an Individualist.*

He wants to express himself too. He wants to accomplish some goals. Let him develop in his own way. As much as you can, tell him what and why, not how. Help him, guide him, but remember he is a unique individual. If he is any good there is no one else like him. Let him develop in his own way. Let him build on his own strengths.

5. *Let the Communication Flow Both Ways.*

A man should "report to" his boss. He should never "work for" him. A man works only for himself and for his family, not for his boss. The relationship must permit a free flow of ideas. You can learn as much from him as he can learn from you. Goals should be set jointly. Opportunities must exist for both.

Set the Stage

Create an environment that stimulates people to try new ways, to take some risks, to make decisions, and to stretch their mental abilities.

Encourage individual initiative and enterprise. Let your people freely communicate with each other. You will develop an excellent team in which each individual will personally put his shoulder to the wheel.

Make people *think*. You can help solve many problems in areas you have no technical skill if you ask the right questions and make people analyze what they already know. Keep probing for answers that fit the technical facts your people give you.

In asking people to do things, do so with an air of expectancy and self confidence. When you ask someone to do something assume it will be done. Act as if it will be done and it *will* be done. Show a doubt and you will get little done for you.

Don't expect your subordinate to know every detail himself and to have all kinds of up-to-date data and information at his fingertips. If you do that you are preventing *him* from delegating as he must run the show himself if he is to know all the details.

Give your people broad leeway. Let them keep redefining their own jobs to meet changing conditions.

A most effective training method is to give people responsibilities and full authority for smaller tasks at the beginning and gradually work up to bigger and more complex operations.

Secure the commitment of all members of your group to the achievement of objectives. Lead each individual to *want* to reach the goals. Make every worker a partner. Consider and accept ideas which are contributed. Give them a sense of participation and you will find their sense of commitment deeply engrained.

Don't Assume

In the matter of delegating and training there is a caution that at first seems contradictory. It fits very well, however, with the fact that you must develop and delegate but you can never give up *your* responsibility for seeing that the job is done.

The very important management motto that I emphasize here is—Never Assume. Never assume what your own eyes, your own ears, and your own mind doesn't tell you is so. Question everything. Take nothing for granted. You can't afford surprises.

Don't assume that everyone (including yourself) is doing everything possible and that nothing more can be done. Remember that in any situation there is *someone* who can do the job. That person may change the factors, juggle them, change a great many things, but he will accomplish the job.

If someone else can do it, why not you? (You must believe someone can do the job, for otherwise you are saying the job can't be done. If you don't believe the job can be done you cannot possibly succeed.)

Correct the Mistakes

You cannot always be right and you cannot always help the man to be productive in your company. There will be times when the right thing to do is to fire the man. It is sometimes the best thing you can do for the man himself.

Most people fit somewhere in the business society. If you have done all you can to help him fit into your organization and he still cannot make it, he needs the chance to fit elsewhere, possibly in another type of business.

The decision to fire must be cold and objective, devoid of

any emotional involvement. He either fits or he does not fit. He is either the right man for the job or he is not the right man for the job. This is a competitive society and every part must be able to compete successfully. If the man cannot help you win, he cannot stay.

Consistently poor or mediocre performance cannot be condoned, let alone rewarded. The man who sets his goals low, or who consistently fails in performance, should not be allowed to remain in his job. He should be moved to a lower job or dismissed. He should never be "kicked upstairs."

This does not mean that people should be penalized for making mistakes. Nobody learns except by making mistakes. The better the man is, the more mistakes he will have made—for he will have tried more new things.

The determination of what you do with the man after the decision is made must be a humane and personal one. The well being of one human is of overriding importance. If there is another place within the organization in which he could perform well, put him there, even if it takes some retraining. If he just cannot fit in, give him as much insight as you can into his problems and help him to solve them. Help him to find the right job. Make his leaving as free from financial hardship as you can.

Firing is part of the hiring process. You usually eliminate the bad ones in the recruiting and interviewing. The few that sneak through and get on the payroll must be eliminated too. Those who don't keep pace with the growth and changes cannot be allowed to hold back the ones who keep working at it.

Make the decision a cold one, but whatever action follows should be warm and humane. This principle will help you to see the facts. It will help you to recognize the need for firing when that need comes up, and will give you the strength and wisdom to handle the situation well.

In a Nutshell

To get results delegate by goals and accomplishments. Let your subordinates develop the best ways to reach those goals. No matter how much you delegate, though, keep close enough to what is happening to make sure the job gets done. Continue to delegate what you've been doing as you learn to do new and bigger things. Continue to free yourself for the jobs ahead. Encourage your people to work directly with others to get things done. There's no need to have everything clear through you.

Take the time to get to know your subordinates, recognize that those who really try to get more done will sometimes make mistakes, encourage them to develop their own personalities and their own abilities.

Don't assume, however, that what you've delegated is going well. Assume nothing unless you know it to be so. Keep close to what is going on. Be an active leader.

When you find you have the wrong man in the job and know you cannot train, direct, or motivate him to work the way you want him to, you've got to change the man or change the job. The decision as to whether the man is right should be cold and realistic. You cannot afford to wear blinders on this one. The determination of what you do with and for that man after he is removed from the job should be warm and sympathetic. Each person, and what he thinks of himself, is of the greatest importance to responsible management.

9

GOOD BOSSES
ARE THE KEY
TO MOTIVATION

The way in which you stimulate, motivate, and lead others will have a lot to do with how far you go. I have known brilliant, capable men who were blocked from reaching the top because they never learned to understand people and were never able to get others to *want* to do things for them.

There are some people whom everyone likes to work for. If they want something done others find it a pleasure to do it for them. They never seem to have difficulty in finding people to do things. You never hear them saying "there just aren't any capable people around who can do a job for you."

What makes these managers a pleasure to work for? It isn't the money. The bad bosses pay the same, and sometimes even more.

Good bosses are usually pleasant. A scrooge does not make a good boss. *You* don't like to work for a scrooge and neither does anyone else.

Good bosses are appreciative. They give that extra something *everyone* yearns for, appreciation. The waitress or the barber who says the loudest "thank you" gets the bigger tips. You feel

better about giving them more and do so when they serve you.
(The other patrons too who hear the loud and appreciative
"thank you's" give more when it is their turn because they too
like to be appreciated.)

Good bosses don't take people for granted. They don't throw
jobs at you with no explanation and expect you to operate like
a machine. They know the kind of work the assignment will
require. When the job is done and is done well they show a
recognition for the good work. People work for more than
money. For just a little more understanding you can get double
your money's worth. Some jobs are more difficult than others.
Some days are tougher. Show you have enough of an interest
in your people to at least *know* they've completed a tough job.

Employees like to feel they work for a man who has a deep,
abiding interest in their well being. You *can* be such a man.

Set the Course and Guide the Ship

The ability and enthusiasm of the man at the helm sets the
course. The entire organization will reflect his strength, his
enthusiasm, his wisdom, and his personality.

The higher you go, the more imaginative you need to be.
The man at the top is the one who gets things done, the one
who points the way. Stir the imagination and enthusiasm of the
people who work for you. Provide the challenges. Help others
to achieve. The inanimate man may make a satisfactory administrator. He will never be a leader.

What your people think you are, they will try to become.
Live with enthusiasm. It's contagious.

The Laws of Leadership

Most people work better by following a good example than
by merely being told what is proper. If the example you set is

not the kind you want others to follow, don't be surprised when they perform poorly.

To be a good manager you must stimulate your people down the line. Get to know as many of the people as you can, not just those organizationally closest to you. You will get a better feel for what is going on and you will be able to more effectively create the kind of organization you want.

One caution, however, when you talk to the men who report to the one who reports to you. Be interested. Learn what you can. Stimulate the employees, but don't supervise them. Say or do nothing to weaken the authority of the man's immediate superior.

A good way to accomplish this is to be sure you mention the man's boss. "Sounds like a good idea. I'm sure Mr. Yoreboss will find this of special interest. I know he's looking for some answers to this problem."

Report to the man's immediate superior anything of significance which you discuss with his subordinates. Continue to show him that he is completely responsible for running his show.

Your responsibilities as a leader includes the obligation to help your people to satisfy *their* drives, *their* needs, and *their* ambitions. Provide the kind of climate that will help your people to grow. Let them shine and become stars too. The quarterback with more stars on his team wins more games.

Employees look to you to lead the way. Nobody wants to sail on a rudderless ship. Somebody has to call the shots and if you are the head of the group, that somebody is *you*.

They want you to understand, but expect you to be firm. A vacillating boss is no leader. A wavering manager causes anxiety and fear on the part of his subordinates. They cannot look to a profitable future if the boss doesn't have firm convictions as to the direction they should be headed.

Act as if you expect compliance. In asking for something to

be done your tone must be firm and polite. It must not contain the slightest question or doubt. *Assume* it will be done, and it will.

A good leader builds loyalty. He does this by being fair and by recognizing the performance of others. He knows that anything which is accomplished is accomplished because the *group* worked toward the goal. Nothing is accomplished single handed —nothing.

Learn to become an even better leader. It is often true that if the boss spent less time in trying to figure out what is wrong with his people and diagnosed *himself,* he will find it more possible to make more changes for the better.

What Subordinates Expect

What do your subordinates look for? How do they size you up? Let's look at some of the factors most people look for:

1. *Integrity.* Above all, the man expects you to be honest with him. Lie to him and he will quickly find it out. If you have something to say, say it. Don't promise what you can't deliver. Promise less and deliver more. When you realize you've been wrong or unfair use the opportunity to show how big you are. The worst thing you could do is to say nothing and hope he will forget what happened. You just can't pretend that things didn't happen. When you are wrong, admit it and go on from there.

2. *Understanding.* Be reasonable. Be flexible. They expect you to be forceful and strong but want you to understand their problems too. Don't set impossible deadlines and impossible goals. If you do, you are either kidding yourself or planning poorly. If they do something well praise them—in public. If you have reason to criticize, do it in private.

3. *Ability.* The people who work for you expect you to be competent. If you are the head of an Inventory Control Section

they expect you to know what it is all about. They expect the Sales Manager to know selling and marketing, and they expect the General Manager to have a pretty good overall knowledge of the business.

4. *Knowledge of Subordinates' Work Performance.* People expect their bosses to know how well they have performed their jobs. This again is part of being appreciated. They feel more secure if the boss knows what they are doing. They will work a lot harder too if they know the boss will know they do.

Some sort of rating is always going on, whether or not it is reduced to formal reports. All employees, all executives, have the question somewhere in their minds: "How am I doing? I wonder what the boss thinks of my work?" When the man asks "How am I doing?" answer him fairly, squarely, and completely.

5. *Control.* Subordinates expect you to control the group. You are the Captain of the ship. They want to feel that everyone will do his part, that you will allow no slackers in the group. Resentment grows quickly when the boss allows some people to "get away with things" and to work in a sloppy haphazard manner. Be the right kind of guy but run a tight ship. Control what goes on in your group. Don't let things just happen as they will. *Make* them happen as you want. Set your standards high, and *live* by those standards.

6. *Help.* In your subordinates' eyes the only real justification for your existence is your ability to help them attain their goals and satisfy their needs. Don't ever become conceited enough to forget this important fact. If they like you it is only in relation to what they feel you can do for them.

Let Them Grow

A good boss must discipline himself to allow some mistakes to happen. You will sometimes see a subordinate head straight for an error. If it is at all possible that he will see the mistake as he gets closer to it, if it is not a serious one, give him a chance to see it and pull out of it himself. This will teach him to think for himself. It will teach him to plan ahead and to think things through.

Allow your people to get the feel of full authority and responsibility for their decisions. If you interfere, they will let *you* run the show. They will assume you have taken over the responsibility, the result being some serious gaps in who does and is responsible for what. If you jump in too fast you risk weakening your subordinates.

Never steal the credit. Give them full credit in fact whenever you can, even if they did only part of the job. Be careful of the phrase "I did it." Chances are you didn't do it by yourself anyway. Stealing the credit will take the steam out of the man down the line who did some work on the project. He will resent your taking the credit for it.

When something is done well give credit whenever you can to those who are responsible for it. Your superiors will be happy to know you are developing other men. They will understand it was your leadership that inspired the progress and your people will work that much harder for you. Most important of all, by being liberal with the praise and the credit you will inspire the group to accomplish much more.

On the other hand, when something goes wrong take the blame. You *are* responsible for everything within your jurisdiction. As far as your superiors are concerned, you might as well take the blame. The reverse psychology here is that your boss will often discount what you say because he sees you feel your responsibility yet realizes you couldn't personally do everything.

It does not mean of course that you should ignore what went wrong. Correct the problem as fast as you can. Look for *what* went wrong rather than for *who* was to blame. You will find the problems that way and will get a lot more accomplished. (If the *what* went wrong is symptomatic of poor management on the part of your subordinates you've got to correct *that* too. I'm not advocating soft, irresponsible, unrealistic, or evasive management on *your* part.)

Help your people to grow into better jobs. Promote on the basis of what they have done and on the estimate of what they can do in the next position. Whenever possible you should be reasonably sure that whenever you do promote a man he can probably later be promoted to the position above that one. Promote men in small steps if possible so that they may learn more and so that you can appraise their continued ability to handle more as they go along. Promoting a man too soon or putting him over his head could hurt his chances to grow. Treat the authority to promote with the greatest respect.

Control the Pressure

In a position of influence you just can't afford the luxury of losing your temper. You might want to make it appear as if you do for some specific purpose, but you can never afford to really lose it. Another word for temper is "control." People lose their temper only when they lose control of the situation.

Emotional blowoff is an unbusinesslike behavior which will earn the disapproval of your associates and your superiors. A manager can never afford to lose his control.

Keep these points in mind:

1. Develop a tolerance for frustration. Few things will go just exactly as you would like. A good manager must have a capacity for tolerance, must be a good sport, and must have a sense of humor and a sense of proportion.

2. Encourage full participation. Let others discuss and question decisions without feeling personally threatened.

3. Continue to question yourself and to question your own motives. Do you find yourself starting to anger at certain things? What are they and why do they bother you? Are you afraid of being questioned? Do you fear losing control?

4. Take care of the situation before it gets to a critical or emotional stage. Make the organization, training, or people changes early. If the man cannot handle the job, change the man or change the job. Don't let it get to the point where things have to blow up all over the place.

5. Don't hold it in. If there is something you don't like, speak up. If it's worth it, fight for it. Nobody likes a jellyfish. If it's a question of giving or getting the ulcers, give them.

6. Learn to relax. When tensions start to mount, drop it all. Do something completely different from what you were working on, even if only for a few moments. If it's more serious than that, take a walk or turn to something you really enjoy. If the tensions keep mounting, take a vacation. You will be no good to yourself or your company if you are always tied in a knot and if you lose control of what you are responsible to manage.

When people meet serious obstacles between themselves and their important goals, they get aggressive. If they are optimistic about their ability to reach their goal, they will often attack the obstacle. This is good.

If they are pessimistic about their own ability, they get aggressive inwardly. They get angry at themselves.

Losing your temper could be a tipoff that you expect to fail at an objective and this itself may encourage the opponent to fight harder. Once you feel defeat, defeat is not far away.

Learn to keep control!

For Power or Progress?

Having the technical ability is not enough to get you to the top. You will need the *leadership* ability too.

The question "what kind of man makes a good leader?" cannot be properly answered. All kinds of persons make good leaders.

It is more significant to ask, "What do effective leaders *do?*" How can *you* become a more effective leader?

The effective leader is the person who helps the *group* to become more creative and more productive.

A lot will depend on how you use the authority which you have. As you use less of your power and authority, those who work for you will gain freedom in action and in decision making. As you use more of your power, your group's freedom will decline.

For most people high earnings do not spell happiness unless the *work* which brings the earnings is satisfying. Think about it and you will find this is true in your own case. The work itself must hold a man's interest, bring him recognition, yield him a sense of achievement, and bring him the consideration and respect of his boss. People want so much to be consulted on problems and to have a part in decisions which concern their work. Nothing which affects people should be decided without some kind of participation by the people who are involved.

Willing cooperation occurs only when work itself is genuinely satisfying. People are *not* naturally lazy. The expenditure of human energy in activity is fantastic. Because of poor management, people often expend more energy in attempting to *defeat* company objectives than they would in *achieving* them. Why? Because of poor leadership!

The important question is not how to get people to expend energy, but how to get them to direct it in the right direction. Management must create conditions to encourage the channeling of efforts toward the objectives of the group. It must create an atmosphere of genuine satisfaction of important human needs and human wants.

The Importance of Recognition

Every man wants to be proud of himself. Everyone wants to feel he is needed, wanted, and is important to someone. No one wants to feel he is just another number on the payroll.

Make people needed, wanted, and important. Make them proud of themselves and their work and they will do an outstanding job for you. Don't take people for granted. If everything is going smoothly in a man's area, don't just let it go at that. Let the man know that you know he is doing a good job. The important trick here is to really *know* that a good job is being done and that takes sincere attention and observation to what your people are doing.

Watch your people at work. Think about their jobs. What does it take to do them well? Some jobs demand concentration. Others demand strength. Notice these things and let people know that you notice them. You will unleash a powerful reserve of energy and enthusiasm to help accomplish the objectives you have set.

Be an "assistant to" your subordinate. You are supposed to help him do his job, not to "direct" him to do it. Pass along reading matter you think he'd be interested in. Show him that you're thinking of him and are interested in his growth. Help him to grow.

The Constructive Side of Leadership

Maintain a cheerful and constructive approach. Develop a positive attitude toward the people who work for you. Believe that your people are capable of doing better work and encourage them to try harder. Put yesterday's failures behind you and start each day with a positive outlook.

Confidence and enthusiasm are contagious. Believing in a man's ability is the best way to help him believe in himself. Appreciate and build up people's good points. Avoid emphasizing the bad. Stress the rewards for doing a good job, not the penalties for poor work. Be patient. Maintain a constructive attitude toward mistakes and misjudgments. Errors are to learn from, not to punish people for. Properly handled, they are assurances of better work in the future.

Look at the constructive side of things. Tell them how to do better rather than just what they did wrong. Avoid negative attitudes and do the positive, constructive thing in all situations. You and your people will get a lot more enjoyment out of the job and you will get a lot more done.

The DO'S and DON'TS of Good Supervision

1. DO find the good qualities rather than the shortcomings of each individual.
2. DON'T give vent to impatience and annoyance at unimportant matters.
3. DON'T hold grudges after disagreements involving honest differences of opinion.
4. DO consider the feelings and *interests* of others.
5. DON'T be overly preoccupied with your own selfish interests.
6. DO help the other fellow at every opportunity.
7. DO be fair—even when it hurts.
8. DON'T take yourself or your work too seriously all the time.
9. DO be genuinely cordial in greeting people.
10. DON'T surround yourself with "yes" men.
11. DON'T emphasize loyalty and cooperation in a way that seems to make disagreement, disloyalty.
12. DON'T play the problem down. If there is a problem, face it. Don't just wish that it would disappear by some magic happenstance.
13. DON'T gloss over serious differences for the purpose of harmony. The problem will explode later with even greater force.
14. DO encourage favorable attitudes by letting people participate in decisions which affect their work.

In a Nutshell

No matter how much power the boss may have, it is the *subordinate* who controls the final decision. It is the one who will *perform* the work that decides how much he will do and how well he will do it. It is the employee, no matter how far down the ladder he may be, who ultimately decides whether to show up for work or not.

A man wants to belong to a group. He wants to be a real part of it. The way you regard him, the way you seek his genuine participation, will influence to a great degree whether his objectives will become the same as yours. Get the group to participate and to feel a sense of authorship for what is done around them. No individual, no matter how he may feel at the start, will go along with you unless his group feels that way too.

Make it worthwhile for your people. Pay your good men well and tell your bad ones off. Pick the right people. The real leader in the group may be someone other than the official superior. Find out who he is and if possible make the real leader the official leader too.

Make it pleasant for each employee to be a member of your team. Give personal attention to each. Encourage cooperation and generate a sense of belonging. Understand employees' problems both on and off the job. Recognize accomplishments.

Treat your subordinates as if they may someday be your boss. Treat them as you would have them treat you. Be on their side, and they will be on yours.

10

THE POWER OF
EFFECTIVE COMMUNICATION

Most of the problems in business can be traced to poor communications!

Subordinates fail to carry out instructions. Managers do not coordinate their plans with each other. The executive expects certain performance but fails to give the necessary orders. One department hires workers while another furloughs them. People speak but no one understands. *These* are the problems of poor communications.

Your prime responsibility is to get things done through people. However sound your ideas or well-reasoned your decisions, they become meaningful only if they are *effectively* communicated to others and only if they achieve the desired action. If you don't get the action you want, you haven't communicated.

The Substance of Communication

Basic to the problem of poor communication is that each person, each of us, lives in a world of his own. No one's world is exactly like that of any other person. What one hears is often different from what the other says. The need is ever present to get through the personal "filters," the barriers, and the mental deafness on the part of those with whom we must communicate.

Don't mistake the *form* of communication for its *substance*. Executives pay too much attention to media and devices and too little to purpose and content. Communication is not a simple isolated problem. It is a complex and dynamic process.

Communication is *understanding*. It is rapport. It is a feeling for the others' point of view. Only when you have that—and that comes only through patient and sincere listening—when you have that you have good communications.

There are few problems too simple, few answers too obvious that one's thinking cannot be sharpened by consulting with others. Participation and effective communications require a permissive climate, sensitive listening, and the willingness to credit others for their contributions. It requires skill in leading conferences so that people could speak freely. It requires confidence in the ability of others to make significant contributions. Effective communication requires a sincere application of the philosophy of "Management by George."

Communication grows best in a climate of trust and confidence. Managers must keep faith with their employees, report facts honestly, and listen sincerely. An employee's knowledge that he has free access to information is as important to him as any specific information you can give him. If your intent is sincere, if your people believe in that intent, then and then only do you successfully communicate.

Your people will be influenced not by what you say but what you *do*. It is behavior which gives meaning to words. Subordinates are not fooled by the boss who says good morning or asks about a sick child unless he really means it. The boss who levels with his people, who listens to their problems, and who is genuinely interested, can exercise effective leadership even though he may sometimes forget to say good morning. An "open-door" policy wouldn't mean a thing to your subordinates if they do not feel comfortable in your office.

The most powerful communication is what you do, not what you say. What counts in the final analysis is not what people are told, but what they *accept*.

Leadership Through Public Speaking

As business gets larger and more complex, as new scientific developments help to speed the tempo of change, it becomes more and more important for business leaders to reach and talk to more people at one time. Good public speaking ability will give you tremendous competitive advantages and opportunities to influence more people.

Anyone who can speak well in private can learn to speak well in public. Only the dimensions of numbers and size have been changed. All the rest remains very much like a conversation between you and an associate. I have seen seemingly hopeless aspirants join a Toastmasters Club and months later turn out to be creditable public speakers. Progress is sometimes slow, but progress there is.

As you go up the proverbial ladder you will need to accomplish goals through an ever-increasing number of people. The most effective way to transmit your beliefs and enthusiasm, and the most practical way to communicate your thinking and getting a feeling for theirs, is by talking with them in larger groups.

To succeed in anything you need to sell ideas. To sell ideas you need to communicate!

Learning to Speak

Join a class or a group. In some cities public speaking courses are given free in connection with high school or college evening courses. Public speaking courses can also be taken at specialized schools such as the Dale Carnegie Schools of Public Speaking.

Toastmasters International is an excellent organization in

which to develop public speaking ability. With headquarters in Santa Ana, California, there are Toastmasters Clubs throughout the world. The dues are nominal. Clubs usually meet once a week during an evening or noon-time meal. The purpose of the club is to have each member help other members to develop public speaking know-how. Everyone is given frequent opportunities to speak before the group.

Prepare Better Speeches

Here are the points to keep in mind in preparing talks that really communicate:

1. *Practice.* Public speaking takes lots of practice. Practice in private before you give a talk. Go over the talk as often as you can. Don't memorize words. The words should be different every time you practice. Know exactly what you want to say, however, and how you want to say it. Practice vocabulary building. Practice voice management, and practice orderly thinking.

2. *Think the Speech Through.* Make sure you understand what you will be talking about before you even start to prepare the speech. Know *all* sides of the question, even if you plan to speak on one aspect of it. Make sure the speech fits the occasion. Make sure your talk is oriented toward your audience's point of view. Have something important to say, something that *must* be said.

3. *Organize Your Talk.* The introduction must get immediate attention, warm up your audience, and get them ready for what you are about to say. What you have to say should be said in the body of your talk. The conclusion should inspire your audience to take the kind of action your speech was designed to influence. It's as simple as that.

4. *Make It Simple.* You want to *communicate.* You want to get ideas across. Your purpose is not to show how learned or erudite you can be. Say what you have to say as simply and as

accurately as you can. Let your talk reflect *you*. Don't change into a different person when you get before an audience.

Really Deliver

Keep these points in mind when delivering the talk:

1. *Establish Contact.* Tune in. Make sure you command attention before you start to talk. Survey your audience before you say a word. Look at them before you start, and continue to appraise them while you speak. Look at specific but different people throughout the talk. Act as if you were talking to one person at a time.

2. *Get to the Point.* Answer the audience's unspoken questions simply, directly, and forcefully. Don't use three words where one will do. Don't use big ones when small ones would be more crisp. A good speaker sits down while the audience wants to listen just a little longer. The poor speaker talks long after his audience has lost interest.

Be sure that what you say is clear. Say it in as many ways as you can. If it needs it, pause sufficiently for the point to sink in. An audience cannot turn back a page if it misses a point. It has to understand the speaker as he proceeds. Don't try to say too much in the time allowed.

3. *Talk With the Audience.* You wouldn't think of talking to a small group of people without looking at them. Your tone and eye contact are just as important when talking to larger groups. Talk as you normally would. Let your natural self come through. Talk as if they were asking questions while you spoke. Answer those questions in your speech. Talk thoughts and ideas, not merely words.

4. *Make It Interesting.* Tell them something they don't already know. If the audience lends itself to it use names of persons in the audience. This is a good attention getter and makes you and your talk more human and more interesting.

Use vocal variety. Build climaxes. Whisper at times. Shift your pace or tempo. Vary the length of your phrases and sentences. Vary your pauses, too.

Never say "uh" or "er." If you have to think, *think*. Make no sound. Your audience has to think of what you *said* while you think about what you are going to say. Remember they are always behind you. Give them a chance to catch up without the distracting "ahs" and "uhs."

Use visual aids. Dramatize what you say. Be a *showman*. Use humor. If you can't tell a joke, don't even try, but show at least that you *can* see the lighter and the human side of things when it seems appropriate.

Speak with sincerity, conviction and enthusiasm.

Create the Opportunities to Speak

You could never get enough practice. Take every opportunity you can to speak in public. If you don't get enough opportunities, *make* them. Volunteer to speak before groups. Speak up at club meetings. (It gets easier after a while.) Learn to think on your feet. The ability to speak in public could be one of the most rewarding skills you could ever acquire.

The Most Powerful Tool in the World

Study words. Make good friends of them. They could be a lot of fun while they help you to communicate your way to success.

Words could help to accomplish difficult tasks. The story is told of P. T. Barnum, the great circus showman. Early in his career he organized a small museum and invited people to come in and look—for a fee of course. One Sunday afternoon the museum was jammed. One more skinny man couldn't fit in. Outside there was a line of people waiting to pay their money to get in. What was P. T. Barnum going to do? He just *had* to make more room so that he could get some more paying customers into the museum. He had to get the people who were inside to leave as quickly as possible.

He had a large sign painted and tacked over a door. The sign read THIS WAY TO THE EGRESS. People saw the sign, turned the knob on the door, opened the door and went through. . . . , They found themselves on the street. They thought the word *egress* stood for some kind of animal. They didn't know the word meant *exit.*

The choice of the one best word helped P. T. Barnum to accomplish what could otherwise have been a very difficult task.

Pick the word that paints the picture. Pick vivid words. To say that "Bill hurried home when he heard his child was ill" is nowhere as vivid and illuminating as saying "Bill *raced* home when he heard his child was ill."

Pick figurative words. To say "the government is *interfering* with business" is not as effective as saying "the government is making a *football* out of business."

Certain words express a point of view. They can prejudice the listener for you or against you. Use the words which carry the punch. There's the story of a man, for instance, who always complained that his wife nagged him continuously for money.

"Nag, nag, nag," he would say to his buddies, "that's all she does all the time. Money, money, money, she's always asking for money."

And the buddy asks after a while, "What does she *do* with all the money you give her?"

"Money? *Who gives her any money?*"

In telling this story from the husband's point of view the word is "nag." Should the wife be telling the story she would use the word "plea." Pick the words that create the image you want to present.

The temperance man would use the words *booze* or *ginmill.* The whiskey salesman would use the expression *cocktail lounge.*

People who look only to the dictionary for the meaning of words proceed under a great delusion if they suppose that what they find in a dictionary is the word's full meaning. What they find is that the dictionary definition of words consists of other words. You've got to be able to feel words and to know the family they belong to, the company they keep, the ideas they conjure up in people's minds, the emotions they evoke, and the results they are likely to bring.

Communication has enabled man to rise above all other beings. Words are the tools of communications. Learn to make words work for you.

The kind of words you use could influence the way you think and the way you influence others. Let words like *exciting, enthusiastic, alive, illumination* become part of your speech.

Realize the *implication* in certain words. You'll never get your boss to go along with a suggestion if you tell him the project would be a good *gamble.* You'll get a lot further if you tell him the project would be a good *investment.*

And just one parting thought while we are on the subject of words. These are mistakes made so often by people who are otherwise well educated. If the people who hear you know you are using either of these two phrases incorrectly, it could be most annoying to them and damaging to you:

The proper phrase is "the reason is *that,*" not "the reason is because." "Reason" *means* "because." Remember—the reason is *that.*

The other frequent mistake concerns the words "imply" and "infer." "Imply" is an outgoing word. It is what you mean to tell when you are talking. "Infer" is an incoming word. It refers to what the listener deduces from what the speaker has said.

Write to Communicate

Write clearly, effectively, and to the point. Good report and letter writing is one of the best ways to call yourself to the attention of the higher-ups.

If you can't state it clearly, chances are you don't really understand it yourself. The expert could explain something in a few crystal clear words. The man who's not really sure will take many sentences to explain.

What you write should reflect *you*. It should sound as you would sound if you were there to say it in person. Business communications must be *alive*. They are supposed to get things done. They are supposed to inspire action.

The value of what you write is measured by how effective it is, not by how many fancy words or trite expressions you use. A business communication should be written as something that means business. The *you* attitude is essential. Even before you dictate the first word, put yourself in the shoes of the one you are writing to. Only by writing from *his* point of view will your communication accomplish its purpose.

What you write should be unmistakenly clear; absolutely sincere and correct; brief and to the point; have the reader in mind; and reflect your character and your personality.

Anything you write should have *one* major idea. If you can't summarize it in one sentence, rewrite it. If it tries to accomplish too much, it will accomplish nothing. No one can consider two major thoughts at one time. You stand to lose the impact of your message if you include too many unrelated thoughts. Business communications are normally filed away when not actively in use. They sometimes have to be referred to different people within the receiver's organization before they can be answered. To include more than one subject on one communication makes it difficult to refer, difficult to file, and difficult to handle.

Ideas should be expressed and arranged in logical order. They should lead the reader smoothly from beginning to end. Wherever possible, start the communication with the reader's problem first and lead from *his problem* to *your suggestion*.

If it's a complaint, conciliate him first and then give the facts and the action you intend to take. If you intend to say yes to a request, say it at the beginning. Say yes as quickly and directly as you can. If you must say no, however, give your reasons first before saying no. Keep the reader in mind and you can't go wrong.

If it's a general communication to a group, whenever practical test your written communication and see how it will be interpreted by the people for whom it is intended. You will be amazed to learn sometimes what the reader makes out of what you intended to convey. Rewrite it so it can be understood.

Remember that communication means what the *reader* thinks it means.

One final emphasis with regard to business writing—what you write must be clear, accurate, and effective. Whether or not it is grammatically "correct" is of secondary importance. One can write with grammatical correctness and yet fail to communicate. Language must be used *meaningfully*.

Feed the Grapevine

One of the earmarks of a good manager is the ability to keep suspicion and rumor to a minimum. Both can be costly. All it takes to arouse suspicion are a few unexplained facts. It is amazing what people will imagine when suspicion is aroused.

People don't keep suspicions to themselves. Something which started as the wildest sort of speculation will be further enlarged and distorted as it passes along the grapevine.

The grapevine is a communication network that operates with extreme rapidity. People who think they know a "secret" find they just *have* to pass it along. How else would they show their importance. "Secrets" are thus passed along the grapevine with astonishing rapidity.

The grapevine is especially fast when the news is significant. The grapevine quickens its pace when people are insecure. Study the grapevine in your organization. How does it work? Who are the key connectors? You will need this information if you want to make effective use of the grapevine for meaningful communications.

Grapevines could be used as "trial balloons." If you would like to know the possible reaction to a proposed course, let the grapevine hear that such a course *may* be in the wind. The kind of reaction you get could help you to determine whether you want to go the proposed route. Learn to use the "calculated leak" to precondition the group to some unusual news which is apt to follow.

To keep the grapevine healthy, to keep suspicions and rumors from developing, here is what you have to do:

1. Conduct yourself in an open and above board way.
2. Keep people well informed on what is going on. The more of this you do the less susceptible your people will be to speculation and rumor. Don't presume your message will be passed all the way down the line. It will be filtered down with bits of the message removed and new slants replaced on the way down. If the subject permits it, talk to as many levels of supervision as you can. Distribute written communications as widely as possible.
3. Be constantly on the alert for things which might be misunderstood or misinterpreted. Explain them before suspicion and rumor can get started. By keeping in close touch with the people you can spot incidents which need prompt explanation.

You can become suspicious too. When you have questions,

whether it concerns the people who work for you or the people you work for, don't speculate. Go directly to the people concerned and get the facts. *Facts kill rumors.*

Get the Feedback

No man is an island. He is part of everything he has seen and heard. He is part of his total environment. He is being changed every day and is changing those he comes in contact with.

You must understand that in order to have any idea at all of what the other fellow may be "hearing" when you say what you think you are saying. He hears it only as it affects him and in the light of his own experiences. If you say it only as it affects you, in the light of your own experiences and without regard to his needs, you won't get through to him. You may blame *him* for not understanding, but chances are that the fault lies with you. If you are the boss, chances are that you have more to learn about communication than does your subordinate.

It is difficult enough for people to convey their thoughts and feelings. Another person can never convey all that he feels, all that is occurring within him. He can only tell as much as words or other symbols will carry. Therefore we can never be sure we know how he feels. Recognition of this fact constitutes the very germ of anything we might call tolerance or human understanding.

Keep your ear to the ground. Get the feedback. Listen to what they are saying if you want them to hear what you say. Listen not only for words. Posture, tone, facial expressions, and gestures can sometimes tell you even more.

Listen more than you speak. Observe what goes on. Seek to improve your beliefs rather than to defend them.

Keep in touch with the grass roots. The higher you go the more important it is that you keep in touch with the needs and the thoughts of the greater numbers of people. Stay in touch with reality. You never rise above that, for when you think you do, you've really fallen below it.

In a Nutshell

To get action through people, you've got to communicate. Develop a permissive environment, a sympathetic ear, and a genuine interest and confidence in others. Remember too, that people will be influenced more by what you do than by what you say.

To get things done through more people and larger groups learn to speak effectively before an audience. Anyone who can speak well before a few people can learn to speak effectively before a larger group.

The right words can open many doors and generate many actions. Learn to use words to accomplish your goals. Good business writing, too, could catapult you to the top. Write effectively and to the point.

Watch the grapevine. It could ruin you or be the means for more effective action. Keep your ear to what's happening and in touch with reality.

11

ORGANIZE
TO GET THINGS DONE

Ability to organize your work and your time will determine how many *important* things you will get done. Many otherwise effective leaders fall down on their ability to organize.

Many men appointed to their first management jobs, fail right there and then. They fail because of their attitude toward what a manager is supposed to be and is supposed to do. They look on the management appointment as a reward for past accomplishments rather than a *challenge and responsibility for future action.*

They look on their job as one who administers and makes decisions, rather than one who takes action and gets things done.

Don't Let the Office Trap You

The office and the desk have kept many managers from growing above the administrative level. If all you want is to be an administrator, recognize the fact. Don't fool yourself into thinking you want to go way up in business. Don't look at yourself as an executive or a leader. If all you want is "to run things," that is all you will be paid for.

Efficient administrators or top level clerks are plentiful. Tell them what you want done, give them a detailed procedure or precedent to follow, and they will see that the job is done. These are not the men industry turns to for imagination, leadership, spark, or growth.

The good executive writes down or mentally notes what he wants TO GET DONE each day, each month, and each year. (Not what he wants to do, but what he wants *to get done*.)

The good executive gets out of the office. He is in the factory, at a customer's office, in a branch office, at one of the sales counters in his store, or any other place where *he* wants to see what is being done and where *he* wants to get something done. In executive management it is indeed true that a rolling stone gets things done while a sitting boulder sees nothing and accomplishes less.

I have been asked by managers why they haven't been promoted to higher positions even though they have handled their current jobs efficiently. You can sometimes handle your present job too efficiently. If you yourself are doing the less important tasks instead of training others to do them, you are not preparing yourself for greater challenges. You should be learning more and can do it only if you teach your assistants to do much of what you are now doing.

You will not be picked for the bigger job unless you are a manager who gets *important* things done. You will be kept at the administrative level if you are so good at it.

An annual salary of $12,000 to $14,000 is a critical one. Few people remain at that salary. This is the point where the administrators are separated from the originators. If you continue to do a clerical or routine job you will stay at that level or perhaps even step back. If you are a business *leader* you will move ahead. To get to the $12,000 level you need to be more efficient on the technical, specialized, and administrative level. To get above that level you need to be more imaginative and dynamic.

Unless you discipline yourself against it, the office could hold you back from getting things done.

Organize for Results

Many executives are constantly plagued by the frustrating thought that they have more work to do and more people to see than they can satisfactorily handle. They recognize that unfinished work on their desks means delayed decisions and interrupted production at lower levels of management.

A time shortage of this kind is a *symptom,* not a problem. A symptom of poor organization!

Organize so that you are free to observe what you want to see rather than to rely on what others want you to see.

Many administrators treat their desks as wastepaper baskets with drawers. Papers which reach their desks are as good as lost. They are never seen again—buried until the opportunity for action is lost. We used to kid an associate some years ago and ask him if there really was a desk under all the papers— none of us ever really saw the desk.

A cluttered and disorganized desk represents a disorganized manager who does not clearly know what should be done and how best to do it.

Scooping the papers off the top of the desk and hiding them in drawers where they will not be seen does not change the picture. The man who occupies that desk has a lot to learn on how to get things done.

Very often *any* decision is better than none. Many organizations have suffered because the man at the top shied away from making decisions. Whether you are a Section Supervisor or a President you have a responsibility for leadership. People have a need for growth and accomplishment and they look to their bosses to lead the way.

There is no such thing as "no decision." "No decision" is

often really "decision by default." You make a decision whenever a problem arises or whenever alternatives exist. Even if you don't say a word, you still have the responsibility for whatever happens as a result of your action or your silence. Whenever alternatives exist, one of the alternatives will be followed, either because the executive so decides or because he allows it to happen by default.

Let us consider several situations as examples:

A recommendation has been made that the Sales Department develop a market new to the company. This will cost money, take time, and compete with some of the company's present product line. Forecasts indicate that sales of the new product will exceed the decline of the old product line, but obviously no one could be sure the forecasts are right.

Several executives disagree as to whether the move would be wise. It finally reaches a point where the Director of Sales must decide "yes" or "no".

He is not sure and lets the matter stand as is for another six months to "see what develops".

If he thinks he made no decision he is terribly mistaken. He decided "no" and that decision will influence certain alternatives including possible loss of growth opportunities and giving to competition a lead in developing what might be a lucrative market.

Another situation might involve an investment of several hundred thousand dollars in new equipment:

The head of Production argues that the investment will lower manufacturing costs. The Sales head feels that a larger advertising appropriation would generate more growth and larger profits. The Financial man warns that if the expenditure does not improve profits quickly the move would hurt financial operating results and the company's future ability to raise capital.

The President is faced with several alternatives, none of which includes the possibility of no decision. If costs are not lowered, or profits improved, the company will face financial difficulties. If the money is spent and no improvements result, the problem would be even worse. He must decide to take that course which is most likely to bring the best results.

Putting the matter off would be the same as deciding not to make either investment and to risk going broke through indecision and inactivity.

This applies to small things too. Minor decisions should be made as the opportunities arise. (I call them opportunities rather than problems because if properly handled most of them *are* opportunities.)

Paper Work

The man who is chained to a pile of paper work day after day and night after night is limited in his creative output. A man's mind may make its most important creative contribution on the night that the briefcase full of work is left at the office.

I referred earlier to the hoarding of papers in one's desk. When a piece of paper reaches your desk you face the following possibilities:

1. Make a decision and communicate it.
2. Request more information or advice, putting the paper in a pending file until a predetermined date or until you receive a reply.
3. Throw the paper out. More paper work belongs in the waste basket than now reaches it.
4. If a decision is not timely but you want to re-evaluate it at a later date, send the papers to the follow-up file.
5. Whatever else you do, get the papers off your desk as quickly as you can. Decide what to do, decide to do nothing, or decide to put it off to a specific future date, but *decide* you must. Get the papers off your desk or they will annoy you, bother you, distract you, and hold you back from accomplishing more important things.

The Follow-Up System

I referred to the follow-up file or follow-up folder. This is one of the most useful techniques of management. Place a date on the upper right hand corner of the papers or correspondence with the letter "F" for "Follow-up." "F 10/5" would mean "put this in the follow-up file and return it to my desk on October 5."

By getting it away from your desk until that time you dismiss it from your mind. You don't have to keep thumbing through it until you are ready to give it serious thought. You do not risk forgetting it by having it lost among many papers in your desk. You don't have it among a pile of other papers, not knowing and always worrying what might be important in that pile and what should be taken care of right away.

A follow-up file permits you to take care of one problem at a time, enabling you to get more work done, and conserves mental energy for more effective work.

Don't Let Red Tape Stop You

The manager whose life is dedicated to paper work has lost the initiative. He is dealing with matters that are brought to his attention. He has stopped finding things out for himself. He has in essence been defeated by his job.

A good executive retains the initiative. He does not allow himself to be chained to his office by a flood of routine nonsense. He anticipates the questions before they get to official reports. He keeps close to what is going on at the front line or grass roots level. He goes out to do something about the problems while they are still small.

At the base of the problem of too much paper work is the tendency to overcentralize. The closer to the problems you encourage decisions and actions to take place, the less paper work you will need done. Let people communicate directly with each other. The organization chart is a tool, not a religion. The more you try to do yourself and the more you try to keep your finger on the pulse of every minute detail, the more impossible it will be to accomplish important goals.

Set the Priorities

Fight the tendency to regard all things as equally important. You should not handle all problems in the order they come to you.

More important, resist the temptation to handle the *least* important problems first. There is a tendency to tackle them right away because they are often the easiest ones to dispense with.

Get to the important things first. If it's most important, spend as much time as you need to solve it. Even if you never get to some of the others, you will be ahead because the meaningful opportunities will have been taken advantage of. Let someone else handle the trivial, or let it go altogether.

Devote most of your abilities to matters that affect future operations, involve more people and broader areas, and are generated by what *you* think should be done. That's the way to get a lot more mileage out of your executive actions.

The least important matters generally are those which involve things that have already happened, pertain to fewer people, or are about matters you were *told* to handle. Avoid spending too much time with those kinds of decisions or actions. You won't accomplish much that way.

Don't succumb to "In-Basket-itis," or the tendency to regard everything that gets to your In Basket as a command that you work on it at all or that you work on it in the sequence in which it reached your In Basket. You can't be much of an executive if you let your In Basket set the pace and determine the rules.

Set priorities. List the most important projects first. Work on the top ones and don't go to the others until you have completed the more important ones. Don't be concerned if you don't finish everything on the list. You will have completed the most vital ones anyway. You will not complete as many *important* things with any other system.

Punch a Hole in It

I had a boss many years ago who taught me a simple but great trick for organizing one's thoughts and one's file when trying to wade through a problem that originated many months and many memos before.

Whenever I came to him with the file on a complicated matter and one with which he was not familiar, the first thing he would do is to take the file apart. He would remove all clips and staples. He would read all the papers from the oldest ones through to the most recent ones. He would throw out extraneous or unnecessary scraps.

He would then punch a hole through the neatly reassembled file and put a file pin through it. By that time he knew the entire story. The neat uncluttered file indicated a neat uncluttered mind who was able to see the important aspects of the problem. To go into his office with a hodge-podge file was like going into the den of a lion who hadn't eaten for three weeks.

Punching a hole in it (or better still training your secretary to do it) will help you to organize your work and make logical decisions.

When You Are Swamped

When you are rushed, slow down!

When you feel you are being pushed so hard that you could never get through all the work, stop! The worst thing you could do is to speed up. You could not possibly do a good job by speeding up. If what you do is going to be measured by how many details and unimportant chores you handle, don't hope to become a successful executive.

When the pressure to do more work starts to mount, stop and decide *what* you will do, how much you will do, and more important, what you will *not* do.

If it is vital to your goals do it and do it well. If it is something which should be done (and can often be done better by someone else) let someone else handle it. If it need not be done at all (and more than you *think* falls into this category) don't do it. Turn it down, throw it away, steer clear of it, or do anything else, but don't let it rattle you and upset you. Don't let it prevent you from doing the important jobs.

Whenever you find you do not have time to do everything you would like to, recognize that you are facing a problem of organization. To solve the problem of executive time, you *must* organize yourself.

The number of hours is one thing everyone is equally endowed with. How you spend them is up to you. You can organize your work and make it pleasurable and constructive instead of energy-sapping and nerve-wearing.

Get rid of present harassments to make room and time for planned personal growth. Delegate more. Demand more accountability for profit and other specific accomplishments.

Set aside sufficient time to approach the task in an unhurried manner. If it is worth *your* doing, it is worth doing well. If you do not have the time to do it well, don't do it at all or make time by dropping something else that is less important to your goals.

If you try to work faster and faster as the pressure mounts, you will find yourself with more and more work to do. You will tire more easily, get confused, make more mistakes, and become less efficient. If your ambition is to become a human machine doing repetitive work, learn to work faster. If instead you want to be a better manager, learn to delegate, to teach, to distinguish the important from the less important, and to get essential things done.

Ask yourself, for instance, "Was the trip necessary? Was it worth the time? Should I have tried to handle the problem myself or could Joe, who is stationed there, have done a better job?"

On the other hand, is it not better to get out to see for yourself and to ask questions? Personal contacts and field trips could often help anticipate situations and save time otherwise lost in writing and reading reports and correcting problems after they come up. There are no pat answers to what you should do, but *think* about them before you plunge headlong into something which will do nothing but prevent you from accomplishing something else which may be even more important.

Unexpected visitors are often the cause of being swamped. If you let them they could tie you up in knots, help you to develop anxiety ulcers, and make it impossible to get to the things you are paid to get done. You've got to learn to get rid of unexpected and unwanted visitors. Don't be bashful about it. Look at your watch. Say you wish you could spend more time and *get up* while you say it. Summarize what has been said, tell what you expect the next step to be, and *get up* and walk him to the door.

Get out of the office as often as you can. Travel time is often the best time for uninterrupted thinking. Being out of the office discourages people from just dropping in without making an appointment because they soon learn you are seldom in.

Don't let unwanted people get in to see you. *You* have to be the manager of your time. You can't abdicate that to anyone else. If it won't help you to accomplish your goals don't let them in to see you. If they do get in, lead them out just as fast as you can.

Let It Cool Off

While on the subject of paper work and correspondence there is one important caution. Never send out in anger a letter written in anger. After you have had it typed, put it away until the next day. If you still feel this is the letter you want to send, do so then.

If you are not so sure this is what you ought to say after a day's reflection, rewrite it. Once the letter is out you can never retract it. It becomes fixed and permanent. You are sure to improve it when you rewrite it.

See it from the reader's point of view. Try to understand his problem.

Much correspondence, incidentally, need not be answered with full letters or full memos. This is especially true on intracompany correspondence. Jot the reply on the margin of the original memo and send it back. Chances are you won't need a file copy. If you do, however, just make a duplicate on your office copier and put that copy in your file. This will save time and costs in letter writing, get the reply out faster, and free your secretary for other work.

Your Secretary Can Double Your Output

Your secretary can be a most important person in your business life. If she is good, and she should be, she could help you to accomplish twice as much by taking many tasks off your hands.

A good secretary can have a decided impact on the outlook and morale of the people in your company. Her cheerfulness and efficiency can be reflected over the telephone, through the mail, and through personal meetings with those who call on you.

A good secretary can answer many of the letters which you

receive. She can buck others to those who are more directly concerned with the problem. She can follow through to see that all letters addressed to you are answered. Let her handle some of the telephone calls, give the information requested, or refer the call to those who are more directly concerned with the subject.

If you permit it, the correspondence load could weigh you down. A good secretary will keep that load to a minimum. Much of what has to be answered over your signature could be answered by her for your signature. If she has been with you for a while she should know exactly what you would do or say in certain situations.

Whatever decision is your responsibility to make cannot be delegated. In fairness to your associates do not expect your secretary to make decisions which you or others should make and do not put her in a position where she is giving directions. She does not have the authority and cannot assume it. All decisions must be made by those to whom the responsibility has been given—yourself and your associates.

Your secretary can take a great load off of your shoulders. She can handle a lot of calls. Those who want to talk with *you* however must be free to do so. Keep the channels of communication open. Know what is going on. You cannot wait until it becomes a major calamity before you hear about it. Your secretary can become an invaluable boss's assistant, but never the boss.

A capable secretary can help you to perform like two people. She can be one of the most important persons in your organization. Don't settle for anything less than a topnotch secretary.

You Can't Do It All

If you tried to do everything everybody asks or expects of you, you wouldn't have time for anything. Do what is important and whatever you do elect to do, do well. Leave yourself enough time to get to the important tasks on time. Leave a breathing spell between each appointment to gather your thoughts, to make some notes, or to travel to your next appointment.

Be an On-Time Manager

You've got to be a manager of time as well as a manager of men. Learn to get the most out of time.

You could never have more time than other people do. The only thing that will help you to rise above others is the better *use* of time.

Develop the habit of being punctual. Don't waste anybody else's time and don't let them waste yours. Be there when you are scheduled. Start meetings on time. It is the only fair thing to do for yourself and the people who show up at the appointed moment. The others will learn very quickly to come to future meetings on time.

Be considerate of other people's time and insist they be considerate of yours. Don't waste a moment of it. You will need all you will get.

Build a reputation as one who gets things done. Be an effective no-nonsense executive, a man who knows the value of time.

Don't dash out at the last moment to keep an appointment. Work back from and around your important tasks. Don't let others or just plain inertia determine what you are going to do next. Do what *you* think is important and what *you* have planned for your day.

Don't waste time visiting with others on the staff. This is one of the most serious causes of wasted time. It is merely a way of postponing a tedious or difficult job. Don't just drift to lunch each day with the same people. It will be more difficult to break away from them later on.

Activity or Accomplishment?

Step back and take an objective look at what you are doing and what you are accomplishing. Are you getting things *done* or merely working hard? What goals are you trying to reach? Where are you now? Success is measured by *accomplishments,* not efforts. Look at the objectives, not the obstacles. Determine *how* the job will be done, not why it cannot be done.

Good organization and good work habits will help to get the job done.

In a Nutshell

Organize for accomplishment. Get close to the scene of action. Anticipate the problems. Let decisions be made close to where things are happening. Organize so that you are free to personally see what is going on. Decisions must be made as you go along. "No decision" is really "decision by default."

Never let paper work become your master. Organize it instead to help you get things done. Do the important things first and do them well. Set priorities in terms of objectives rather than in terms of which piece of paper reaches you first or which situation is first brought to your attention.

The clock ticks on. You can't afford to drift through time. Do each day what *you* decide to accomplish and what will help you most to reach your goals.

12

LET YOUR BOSS
HELP YOU

*Your relationship with your boss and your asso-*ciates will have much to do with how well you can accomplish your job and how rapidly you will be promoted.

The opinions of a few associates, whether they are at the same organizational level, above your level, or below it, can affect the kind of progress you make. People are generally anxious to put in a good word for someone they think is doing a good job. By the same token they don't want to see a phony or incompetent move ahead and will make their opinions known.

The way you impress and react to those around you in business is something you should be alert to and something you should work on. The right kind of personal public relations is part of the game.

Most important of course is your relationship to your own boss. He is the man who will have most to say as to how you progress. If you let him, your boss can help you considerably.

What Is the Boss Looking For?

Let's consider first what your boss looks for in evaluating how well you do your job and who should be promoted to greater responsibility. The factors are no different, you know, from what you consider in evaluating *your* subordinates:

1. How well are you doing your present job? Do you accomplish the goals which have been set? Are you making quick progress?

2. Do you work with enthusiasm and drive? Are you dedicated to the job? Do you keep going in the face of obstacles and discouragement? Do you display a "can-do" attitude? Do you feel an urge to get things done?

3. Do you exercise good judgment? This is extremely important in considering whether the man will be promoted. Do you think things through before plunging ahead? Do you see and understand the broad picture—the relationship of your work and your department to the whole company? Can he trust you to handle the job on your own? Does he have confidence in you?

4. Are you loyal to the company and cooperative with your boss and your associates? This doesn't imply being a "yes" man. Unless you have a mind of your own and unless you contribute ideas for growth you're not much good in the higher job. Modern management, however, is team management, and your boss must have people he could work with and people who could work with others.

5. Are you a good leader? Do you guide and motivate others to full effectiveness? Do you have the stature, self-confidence, control, outlook, and bearing which would indicate you can be placed in the higher job with full acceptance by all?

6. Are you a good administrator? Does your department run smoothly? Do your people know their jobs? Do you organize your work, know how to delegate, follow up, and control? Your boss will certainly not move you up to the next job unless and until you seem to have your present assignment completely in hand.

7. Are you a self-starter? Do new ideas, new trends, and new concepts radiate from you? Can you give some fresh direction to the organization in keeping with changing times and changing opportunities?

8. Perhaps most important of all, do you really *want* the promotion? Have you set your own sights high enough to make it obvious that you are head and shoulders above the others? Are you realistically ambitious? Do you know where you are going? And . . . . have you *prepared* and trained yourself for the next job?

Treat It as Your Own

There is one principle which could guide you well in your relationship with your boss. This principle will help you to make the right decisions and to accomplish more. THINK, ACT, AND WORK AS IF IT WERE YOUR OWN BUSINESS.

The answer to "What would I do if it really were my own business?" is usually the answer you and your boss want. Make sure you are honestly answering that question. Would you *really* take the proposed action if the money were coming out of your pocket?

Treating it as your business has another advantage. It enables you to see the essentials more clearly. It enables you to cut through the organizational maze. It prevents you from viewing procedures, accounting forms, administrative systems, advertising programs, and the many other functions a business organization performs as ends in themselves.

No matter what kind of business you are in, keep always in mind that the elements of the business are very simple. You decide what product to make, you make it, sell it, and get paid for it. That is all that is involved. This is true no matter how big the business gets.

Who Do You Really Work For?

Who do you really work for? This is not a simple question and the answer to it will guide you well in what you should do and how you can grow.

You work for many people. You work first of all for the man you call "boss," the man you report to. You owe him your loyalty and your help. You try to do what he asks of you. You cannot however try to second guess everything you think your boss will want. If you are going to be worth anything as an executive, you will have to do most of your planning and your work on your own. To do that well you have to have a broader sense of direction.

How well you assist in carrying out corporate objectives will determine how high you will go in the corporate organization.

A broader approach protects you against frequent management changes above you or from whims by a few as to what should and should not be done. It identifies you with the company rather than with specific groups or factions in the company.

You work for your immediate boss. You work for his bosses. You work for the Board of Directors. You work for the stockholders . . . and you work for the community. That which is *consistent* among all of these groups is what you work for.

The Kind of Politics Which Pays Off

What about company politics? This is something which all new managers wonder about. This is something that is dramatized in movies and novels.

In the sense that company politics refers to siding or lining up with one group or clique against the other, my advice is to stay out of company politics. It won't help you or your company. It will force you to defend positions which are unwise or unworkable. You will never develop loyal business friends through the use of office politics.

If you will think and act as if it were your own business and try to do what is good for the business, you will have no trouble with company politics. Decide the issues on their own merits and only as they will affect the business. Stick to your own job and your own responsibilities. Work hard, be sincere, accomplish the goals, and you will make good progress. Don't look for cheap personal gains by siding with one group against the other. Anything you get that way will be short term and quite risky. Be yourself and do your best for your company and those you are responsible for.

In management, today, you must be a team player. Resist any temptation to criticize your associates to your superior. He is often aware of their faults and will think less of you for trying to take a personal advantage of it. Forget the competition. Let them take care of themselves. You will be judged by how well *you* do.

Keep the vindictiveness and jealousy out of it. If you do have something to say, say it and leave it at that. State the facts only. Keep the sting out of it. This kind of attitude will encourage greater cooperation from all of your associates—the good ones and the not-so-good ones. You will have more people helping *you* and pulling for *you*. You will be the impartial serious no-nonsense guy your boss wants to promote.

When plans or actions are discussed or if a past action is being analyzed, stay away from the "who's." Don't ask who did this or who said that. Be concerned with the "whats" and the "whys." Leaving personalities out of it will help to get things done.

Forget the position you took last month or last year. Keep an open mind. Be receptive to new facts and new developments.

Don't stick to a point of view long after you have been convinced another point is more appropriate. When people say "but that's not what you felt last month when we talked about it," or "at the meeting in November you said you didn't want to do that" take the attitude that "I learn more each day and this is the way I think *now*," or "the fact that I took such a position then is no reason why I can't re-evaluate it now. I may have been wrong then or conditions may be different now." Look for what is best *now*.

All right. *You* know what to do and how to act. If you are responsible for other people, however, you want to be on the alert for jealousies. Internal politics do develop. Conditions within the organization often encourage men to form cliques. A weak manager often encourages a power play within his department. If you do not get around to your people and are not in constant touch with them you will not be aware of these. Be fair in your treatment and evaluation of your people. Make your selection as much as you can on objective criteria, on how well the people meet stated goals. Make sure *you* are not developing a "fair-haired boy." An executive who takes little time to work with each one of his team encourages the forming of cliques.

Again, as for yourself, forget the personal competition within the company. You are in competition with yourself only. You have to better yourself. Ignore the competition. *You* become the competition by improving all the time. If the others are good they should be promoted. It is in your interest to have capable men at the top of your company. If they are not good they will defeat themselves.

You will meet many small people in life. People who are so petty and so sour that you can't do anything to get through to them. Forget them. Ignore them. Pass them up. Stay away from them. Let them stay on the local track while your express whizzes by. You can't change them so why risk their contaminating you or slowing you down?

What If You Goof?

Samuel Butler once said, "There is no mistake so great as that of always being right."

You will make mistakes. Some of them may be out and out blunders. If you handle them right they could be opportunities in disguise. If you run for cover, look for people to blame, and otherwise botch the situation, it could ruin you.

When you goof or when you are criticized, try to look at the situation objectively. As much as you can, take yourself out of the situation. What really did happen? Was it wrong? What went wrong? Why?

Face the facts. Don't try to run away from them. Don't try to deny what happened. Make an honest effort to get all the facts, no matter who it may embarrass. Assume that everyone tried to do what is best, even if it did not work out just right.

When you hear of a complaint, drop everything else and correct what went wrong or start the correction machinery in motion.

When you are criticized or when you goof stick to the facts. When you try to explain what happened, don't try to lie your way out of it. If you stick to the facts your boss will understand them and sympathize with you more than if you try to sell him an untrue story or give him weak excuses.

Get on your boss's side and try to correct *what* went wrong.

If you lie you will be setting a trap for yourself. One lie will lead to another. Don't try fast talk either. Rapid chatter is quickly recognized as an attempt to conceal what one is afraid might be discovered if one spoke more slowly. It is an obvious cover up which should not be resorted to. If you are wrong, admit it, and try to find the right answers.

Don't blame anyone. The worst thing you can do when you receive a complaint is to let it break down confidence in your department, your associates, or yourself.

Devote attention to *what* went wrong rather than who is to blame. (The *what* went wrong may be that the wrong man was put in charge of a project and correcting it may mean removing the man. In that way alone can a *who* be a *what*.)

Look for solutions, not scapegoats. By looking for the what of the situation, you ally yourself with your boss in search of a common problem—the cause of the complaint.

It is bad to blame assistants or subordinates for mistakes. Nothing will lower you in your boss's eyes more than to blame a subordinate. By criticizing subordinates you are in effect placing the blame on your own shoulders without the advantage of seeming big about it. You are responsible for your subordinates. You hired them and trained them. Don't blame others for mistakes. Look for the facts, causes, and solutions.

If it's not a big mistake don't make a big deal of it. Don't make a Federal case out of it. If you've done something wrong admit it right away. Disarm the other fellow. Say "I goofed on that one" and go back to your job of managing, directing, and growing. Don't let it get you down. All people who accomplish things make occasional mistakes. Your boss expects you to make some. It's how you react to them that counts.

The Boss Wants Results, Not Problems

Here's one where so many managers fall down. Too many are too quick to bring problems to their bosses, rather than solutions and results. The boss isn't really interested in receiving any more problems. He's got enough of them now.

When you receive a complaint from a customer, for instance, don't do as so many do. Don't say, "If you are not satisfied why don't you write to Mr. Bigboss?" *You* might be impressed with the stature and importance of the big boss but the complaining customer doesn't even know his name. Why channel the complaint to him? Take care of it *yourself* if you possibly can. Take the brunt of the complaint. If you need more information, get the information and call the customer back. Don't buck the complaint or the complainer to your boss. It won't help *you* with the boss at all.

Get in Good With the Boss

Management is not a one-shot affair. You will have to work with the same people over a period of time. You will continuously be evaluated and re-evaluated by your superiors. They will never be sure of just how much you can do. How could anyone be sure where people are involved?

Dramatics is sometimes called for. A "can-do" attitude is vital. Reliability is even more important. Are you the man your boss can rely on no matter what job you are asked to do? Could he rely on you to follow through all the way?

The man who seeks more responsibility usually gets it. Take more off your boss's shoulder.

To gain the confidence of those about you promise less than you think you can do and do more than you promised. You might lose out the first time to the guy who promises a lot more, but you will overtake him when he falls flat on his promise.

This practice will allow for unpredicted obstacles and eliminate the need to apologize and make excuses when the job is not completed as planned. It keeps you in a positive position, rather than on the defensive. If you go all out to accomplish the job after it has been promised you will deliver sooner than anticipated or more than expected.

You can be a hero more often if you promise less than you can deliver and deliver more than you promise.

Communicate Upwards

Be a "completed staff work" man. See the job through to the end. Take on more responsibility. Don't keep coming back for approvals on every detail, *but keep the boss informed.*

Keep the boss advised of the significant actions in your department. Let him know the projects you are working on and the progress you are making. Give him a chance to comment if he wants to. Keep forging ahead with your program, making obvious progress all the time, but feed the lines of communication.

A monthly report to your boss telling him what you have done, what you are doing, and what you plan to do is a desirable thing. Do it even if he hasn't asked for one.

To get him pulling for you and to get his meaningful help on the more important projects, he has to be aware of the developments that led to the present situation or opportunities. He has to be able to see it in the sequence and from the viewpoint that you saw it. Ideas must be sold. You can't always ask the boss to do something for you. You have got to *sell* him.

Put yourself in your boss's place. What would you really want done and what would you be looking for?

Bring to your boss's attention any matter for which he may be responsible. Put him in a position to answer questions which may be asked of him. Ask *yourself,* what contributions are you making to the larger unit of which you are a part—to your boss's area of responsibility.

Be a source of new ideas and fresh thinking for your boss. You are closer to some of the problems and to the day to day operations of the business. You are closer to the customers and to the rank and file employees. Your suggestions and your ideas are important to your superior. Present ideas. Give your point of view, but don't belabor a point. There is nothing more annoying and more obstructive than a subordinate who keeps repeating the same request long after the boss has indicated a different course. Some people mistake the locking of one's mind in collision-course with an illusion of independence and individualism. Don't beat a dead horse. Don't belabor a point for which the timing is bad. Seek constantly to *improve* your point of view rather than to defend or push an unworkable or obsolete idea.

Get Yourself a Raise

Money isn't everything, they say, but it could sure buy a lot. Raises help you buy more and are tangible milestones in your executive growth.

Here are a few pointers to help fatten your paycheck:

1. The best way to get a raise or a promotion is to *get your boss a promotion.* What he makes will to a large degree determine what the company will pay you. Help him all you can in *his* executive climb.

2. Another good way to get a raise is to *let the man below you help to push your income up.* Get the best men you can. If your subordinate is so good and if he is paid so much and if you contribute even more, it follows that your income will have to keep going up to keep above that of your subordinate.

When I was a General Sales Manager some years ago I got for myself a substantial raise by finding a top man to run our largest Branch and paying him exactly what I was then earning. The inequity became so obvious, I found a larger figure in my pay check shortly afterwards.

I am not implying that you should pay more than the man is worth. I would consider this to be poor judgment. What I am saying is to go out and get the *best* man you can get and pay him what he is worth. You then will receive what *you* are worth. By paying more your company will earn more, and so will you.

3. To get a raise make sure you *get things done.* Accomplish the job you are assigned to and accomplish it well. Do it so well that there would be absolutely no question of how outstanding you are. Keep your eye on the objectives and the goals.

4. *Continue to improve* your skills and your ability. Listen with your eyes and ears. Make sure you know what is going on around you. Keep in tune with the needs of the organization. Learn all you can about your job and the jobs above you. Recognize your shortcomings and work on them.

One final word of caution. Don't be impatient. Bide your time. If you can possibly avoid doing so, never ask your boss for a raise or a promotion. Make him aware of your interest or your need, but let the idea come from him or seem to come from him. I have seen several otherwise good men blow up their business career by repeatedly insisting they should be promoted then and there. These were men who were pegged for promotion, but were too stupid to bide their time.

Disconnect the Panic Button

What should you do when word comes down from the top that "too many people have been coming in late" or "they have been abusing sick leave?"

The *last* thing you do is to immediately crack the whip and take it out on the very next guy you catch coming in late.

Have more confidence in yourself than to react in that way. Take to heart the complaint that discipline appears lax but look into each situation before you jump. Maybe the man you catch was late for the first time in many years. Don't make an example of *him.*

Don't panic. Don't get all of your people upset just because you are upset. Go about your task in a sensible way. By diving into a headlong attempt to do your boss's bidding you could be upsetting everything to the point of creating more problems for your boss to complain about at a later date.

Do what the boss wants, yes, but use your head. That's what a manager is supposed to do. Be directed in the long run by what the objectives are rather than by the whim of the boss. You're in business, not the Army. Treat your boss as an associate, not as a First Sergeant. You'll get a lot more accomplished that way and he'll feel a lot more confident in you.

Don't Be So Defensive

If you learn to handle this one you've practically got it made.

When somebody seems to be finding fault with you don't arch your back and point your claws. Don't be quick to meet the fight head on. Don't be like a stubborn bull who just won't give an inch.

The harder you fight the fiercer the criticism will become—and more important—the less likelihood there would be that whatever is wrong will be corrected.

Take Yourself Out of the Situation

It is a *situation* or a *fact* that is being discussed, not you. Mentally move over next to the one who is finding fault. Jump right over next to him. *Both* of you look at the problem at the same time from the same point of view. Look for the problem and look for the solution.

Deftly turn the attention away from you to the problem, not by fighting it head on (you only make it worse that way) but by directing everyone's attention to the more likely reasons for the problem.

When the fault seems to point toward you your attitude should seem to say "you've got a point there." "I see how so and so may have felt that way." "We may have a problem there or it may be a matter of communications." "Let's analyze this thing for a moment." "I will keep my eyes open for that." "I will talk with Jim to see what could be done to avoid this kind of thing."

Don't get defensive—we are always a little bit at fault. *Join* the attack and channel it to the problem. Join them in looking for solutions rather than scapegoats.

Put Your Boss on the Team

An effective leader must be able to influence those above him as well as his subordinates. His authority over his subordinates, his ability to persuade them, depends on their recognition that he can persuade top management on their behalf when circumstances call for it.

Avoid being a strictly "top-oriented" executive. Be as conscious or concerned about the actions and attitudes of your associates and your subordinates as you are of your superiors.

Don't be over eager to be at the beck and call of your boss. The puppy who wags his tail and jumps whenever his master comes into the room isn't the one who is asked for recommendations and decisions.

You don't really please your boss by imitating him, jumping at his word, laughing at his jokes, and doing everything to curry favor. He *is* your boss. Treat him as such. Help him to get his job done, but remember you can help most by paying attention to what *you* are supposed to get done.

Give your boss what he *needs* to do his job well. Give him what he needs in the way he wants it.

Visualize what *you* need and want as a boss. Try to visualize what you would need and want if you were in your boss's shoes.

Note the men he promotes and those he does not promote. This could be the best tip off you will need. If you think it appropriate, *ask* him outright what he wants and what he expects of you.

Don't do what some very foolish would-be ladder climbers do. Don't *compete* with the boss. (Many people do just that.) If you are assigned as an "assistant to" be just that. *Help* him and he will help you.

You will sometimes have a temporary boss. You may be on a committee or a special assignment. It may be a community or industry association project. Even though your positions may normally be equal, or perhaps reversed, when the other fellow is put in charge, work for him as though he were really your boss. It's the only way to get things done.

There is no room for dissension in group management. Differences of opinion, yes, but not dissension. A position should be argued, presented, and sold in every way possible until the boss, the man whose decision it is to make, or the majority of the group, decide. Once the decision is made it should be carried out wholeheartedly and energetically by all—even those who had argued a different point of view. If you can't go along at that point quit your job. You won't be any good to yourself or your company beyond that point.

In a Nutshell

Your boss is the man who will have most to say on how you progress. The qualities and accomplishments your boss looks for are no different from those you expect from *your* subordinates. The one great principle that will guide you well is to treat your job as if it were your own business.

Observe the normal courtesies of business but don't play favorites. Be guided only by what is good for the company, rather than by *who* thinks what. That's the only kind of office politics which pays. If you make a mistake admit it quickly and get back to getting things done. The boss has enough to worry about without having to do your job too. What he's looking for from you is progress, not problems. Get things done, but keep the boss informed. Give him a chance to help or change the course, but don't wait for him to do the job. Keep up progress at the fastest rate you can. Get the boss on your team and you will continue to grow and prosper.

13

NOTHING HAPPENS UNTIL YOU MAKE IT HAPPEN

Let's talk about those things which separate the men from the boys in the field of business leadership. What determines whether a man will be a clerk, an administrator, a manager, an executive, or a top-flight business leader?

A top executive has the vision to see what could be done and an intense *need* to see it done. To see it through you need all the determination, stick-to-it-iveness, and good judgment you are capable of mustering. You need to know in what direction your organiation *should* be going and must drive persistently toward that goal. You must have a clear picture of the exciting horizons which are ahead.

You Are on Your Own

The higher you go the less briefing you will get—the more your boss will rely on *you*.

You will not move up fast as long as you rely on your boss for day to day directions. If you feel you don't see your boss often enough, chances are you are not ready to assume greater responsibility. You are looking for too much day to day direction.

The secret is to plan ahead. Know what will be needed next month and next year. Prepare yourself for what you will need to know. Set the direction and pattern for what happens in your department. Communicate more freely with other department heads. Be on your own.

Decision making will be lonely too. No matter what kind of advice you receive the final decision is yours and yours alone. *You* will stand or fall with it. See that *you* make it.

Don't let yourself fall under the spell of inaction by refusing to act until you know all the facts. You will never know them completely. Facts have a way of changing. They have a way of appearing different, depending on one's point of view. Learn to take some risks and to make some assumptions.

Learn to stand on your own two feet and learn it early in the game!

The Hazards of Playing It Safe

Every successful enterprise started with an idea and a man who was willing to take risks to make that idea work.

Just as they are vital in starting a new company, risks are necessary in keeping that company on the path to growth. No organization can stand still. It moves ahead or falls behind.

"Playing it safe" is often the most dangerous course you can follow. Changes will take place all around you no matter what you do. Failure to adjust to changes because of an unwillingness to assume a risk will put you further out of step to the changes taking place. Seeming to play it safe therefore is often the surest way to run into trouble. Fear of assuming small risks now will increase the need to assume larger and potentially more dangerous risks later.

Business was built by competition and it lives by competition. The willingness to take a calculated risk and work to make it pay is indispensable to success.

IBM's Thomas J. Watson Jr. wisely said not long ago "If you can do constructive thinking along unorthodox lines in business, you've got it made." There is a lot of room up there for the imaginative executive who has the courage of his convictions—the man who is willing to stand up and be counted.

Administrative skill is essential for an effective organization. The competitive or scrappy company, however, never puts into top decision-making jobs, executives whose talents are purely administrative. Good administrators can be hired by the dozens. Decision makers and action takers are harder to find. The man who can weigh the facts, decide on the best course, and follow through to see that it gets done has many opportunities waiting for him.

Here are a few suggestions which will help you develop into a top executive:

1. *Don't "play it safe" by hiring people who are sure to fit,* people who know how to stay out of the limelight and out of trouble. You want subordinates you can work with and ones who can get along with others. Of course you do. You do not however want people who are molded into pre-conceived ideas and who are afraid to think for themselves. They won't get you into trouble right away but they will in the long run. The ones who speak up and do some independent and creative thinking will help you to accomplish much more.

2. *Do not depend on formal management-development programs to the exclusion of on-the-job performance.* The best management development program is the one you develop and tailor make for yourself. Learn all you can on whatever interests you. Be curious. Learn about the jobs above you, not the details, but the broad requirements. Read a lot. There is so

much available for *you* between the covers of many books. Attend seminars. Meet and talk with people you can learn from. Subscribe to the papers and trade magazines with the higher business standards and broader philosophy. Reading the *Wall Street Journal* will help you on the way up, the *New York Times* will make you a more interesting person. *Fortune, Harvard Business Review,* and a host of others should be among your reading habits if you want to assume a professional standing in management. Use your lunch hour to best advantage. Spend it whenever you can with people who are stimulating and success-oriented.

3. *Avoid Follow-the-Leader policies.* Examine everything. Ask "why." Remember that *every* business consists of nothing more than making the product, selling it, and getting paid. No matter how large an organization may be, everything should be directed to accomplishing these simple tasks at a profit. Relate all actions to the main objectives. You will cut through a lot of red tape. You will get a lot more done with a lot less effort.

4. *Don't hide behind generalities.* Speak up. Call a spade a spade (but do it nicely). Be completely honest with *yourself.* You will contribute a lot more that way.

5. *Make commitments.* Commit yourself and your people to accomplish more. Take the risks. Lead the way. Your job is leadership—and leadership requires the taking of risks. Play it safe by forging ahead of all the others. Remember that it isn't that the few who succeed are so capable; it is often that the many who do not succeed perform at a fraction of their native ability. You've got no competition at all if you really try.

6. *Seek to learn, not to defend.* Keep an open mind. Don't be blinded by what you would rather think. If the problem is inferior products, what's the sense of putting the emphasis on improving the marketing group? If management is weak, why not strengthen it or improve it? In looking at problems, let the

chips fall where they may. Find the *real* causes and work on them.

7. *Stop the Buck.* Adopt the kind of philosophy which says "the buck stops here." Don't go running to someone else to share the responsibility whenever a problem arises. Become known as the man to come to for a decision. Cut down the activity and build up the output.

Step Way Out

Bold thinking has often been the reason why some businesses have forged ahead. Men at the top play to win. Like the quarterback who is trailing 13 to 14 in the last few moments of the game, who is faced with the alternative of kicking for one point after the touchdown or running or passing for the more difficult-to-make two points, if he is any good he will try the harder and more risky two-point play. These are the kind of men who win football games and these are the kind of men who build industrial empires.

Some companies have staked all they had and all they could borrow on processes or products nobody else believed in. This is the kind of stuff that success is made of. Bold decisions to reduce transistor prices from $16.00 to $2.50 to get a broader and more profitable market, the extension of warranties from one year to ten years, these are the kinds of risk taking actions that put companies on top. The men involved weren't gambling. They *knew* their business. They *believed* in what had to be done. Most of all, they had the *guts* to play for the top!

Look for opportunities, not security. If the job seems safe and secure, chances are it holds no challenges. Chances are it will in the long run not pay half as well as something more risky but more dynamic. Go where the need is the greatest, where the challenges are more intense, and where the risks are greater. Go where the ultimate rewards are a lot more attractive.

There Is No Limit

They used to say the sky is the limit, but even that has changed. Space age conquests have taught us the shortsightedness of placing limits to the horizons of imaginations. *Anything the imagination can see, man can accomplish.*

And so it is with your own personal or business life! The horizons you set, the goals *you* think are possible, will determine how much you accomplish in your productive lifetime. It is true here, as in many other areas, that you are what you think you are, and what you *think,* you are.

People are limited more by their own minds than by physical or external factors. They fail because they didn't think it could be done in the first place.

Break the shackles. Work on the basis that anything which can be imagined can be done and that you are the man who can do it.

"If We Had"

Beware of the "if we had" complex. Few situations are perfect. It is professional suicide for a manager to say "if we had more time we could develop the people we need," "if we had better equipment we could submit the reports they want," "if we had more space we could organize to get the work out faster."

Learn to use what you have and use it well. Find the advantages in what you have.

Your product and your organization has many unique superiorities. Everything could be accomplished by someone. Determine to be that someone.

If anybody can forge ahead with the set of circumstances you have to work with, you can too. Whenever you think a task is impossible ask yourself, "Is there anyone in the world who could do this job?" If the answer is "yes," and it usually must be, then you could do it too. You can often find the specific way by asking, "If so and so can do the job, *how* would he accomplish it?" You would be amazed how often this technique works.

If you let the "if we had" complex get you, it could be deadly.

Make the best of what you have. Turn it to your advantage. Look only for what can be done with the facts as they appear *now*. Monday morning quarterbacks don't make good executives.

Look for Solutions—Not Scapegoats

When something goes wrong take the opportunity to show how big you are and how good you are. Instead of criticizing someone in your company, the fellow who is making the complaint, or the policies within which you have to operate, look for more opportunities to sell what you are trying to accomplish. It will be a lot easier to deal with problems in the future after you have succeeded in establishing yourself as being fair and reliable.

It is a good principle never to blame anyone. The worst thing you can do when you receive a complaint is to let it break down confidence in your department or your company, your associates, or your subordinates. To do that would be to work *against* everything you have tried to do to build the image of a top man running a top organization. You cannot sell them if they don't have faith in your group.

Attention should be devoted to *what* went wrong rather than who is to blame. By looking for the *what* of the situation, you ally yourself with your superiors in search for a common problem—the cause of the complaint.

It is just as bad, and perhaps worse, to blame assistants or subordinates for mistakes. Nothing will lower you in your associates' eyes more than to blame a subordinate. People have a high sense of fairness and support for the underdog. They resent hearing criticism of people who are not present to defend themselves. They resent criticism of other employees or subordinates.

By criticizing subordinates you are in effect placing the blame on your own shoulders without the advantage of seeming big about it. You are responsible for your subordinates. You hired them. You trained them.

Never blame others for mistakes. Look for the facts, causes, and solutions.

What's in It for Them?

To get things done you must give others a driving reason to accomplish. Make it worth their while. Ask always, "What's in it for them?"

Give them stimulating goals to shoot at. That perhaps is more important than some of the ordinarily accepted money and fringe incentives. Men will do what they can conceive of doing. Whatever the mind is stimulated to imagine, man will do. Give them the leadership they need. Give them the dream to work for. Help them to transfer the ideas into reality by making sure the rewards are worth the effort. Take your people into partnership. Let them get a piece of what you yourself are working for. Make sure they have compelling reasons to want to get things done.

Just as the carrot must be there for them to reach, the stick unfortunately is important too. Reward good performance but recognize poor performance too. The men who get things done should be promoted and paid more. The ones who drag the group down should be eliminated. Weed out the poorest five percent (in all categories and grades, not just the lowest paid group), train, develop, and upgrade those who want to grow, and recruit at all times for better people. That's how to develop a big league, top notch, *winning* team.

It Must Be Sold

Could you think of any great leader in any field at any time who was not a good salesman? There never has been and probably never will be a leader of men who makes things happen who is not also a good salesman.

To make things happen you've got to SELL. A business leader is a *salesman*. He is a man with vision, understanding, leadership, and the ability to sell others on what he thinks should be done.

No matter what specialty you are in, if you want to get to the top, learn to sell. Study salesmanship in every way you can.

You must make people *want* to do what you thing they ought to do. No matter how much authority you have, no program will be successful unless you can *sell* it.

To sell something you've got to consider the other's point of view. What's in it for him? How is he likely to see it? Will it make his task easier or more difficult? What will he gain from it?

Present it from *his* point of view and you will have him sold.

If you sincerely consider your proposal in the light of what it will mean to the other fellow you will have a better chance at success.

What you propose may not always be in the other person's interest, but if you *think* about his viewpoint, his needs, and act for the welfare of the entire group, you will have a better chance of selling it.

If you act without considering the other person's viewpoint, you are sure to fail.

Study human behavior and psychology, some of it from books, but mostly from people. Read books on selling. Talk to successful salesmen (even if their titles are Controller, Manufacturing Director, or President).

Selling is a matter of attitude and understanding. It is a matter of *caring* what the other fellow thinks. Everyone can learn to sell.

In selling an idea, if you have to get the approval of others, ask "which" not "if." Which, when, and what are more positive. You *expect* to get approval, you believe in your idea, so why ask "if"? You want the others to know you have confidence in your plan and that you expect it to go through. You want them to know they are expected to say "yes." People like to do what is expected of them.

Let them decide, if they must, on some of the minor details of the plan, but if you are sold, *think, talk, and act as if you expect the plan to be adopted.*

You can learn a lot about sales psychology from watching children. Psychologically, adults are children who have matured or who have learned to hide their feelings and emotions. Adults react just as children do.

Children whose parents expect good results—whose accomplishments parents often praise and seem proud of—act the way they are expected to act. Children whose parents are overly critical, who seem to point out all the bad things their children are capable of doing, also act as they are expected to. Grown-up people also generally do what is expected of them.

If you imply to your associates that you expect them to agree by talking and acting as if they will, your associates and superiors will buy. Express a doubt, by words, tone, or attitude, and your idea is dead.

To make things happen, you've got to sell.

Everything depends on people believing that it could be done and that it will be done. It's as simple as that.

In a Nutshell

Set your sights. Then work to make them become a reality. Stand on your own two feet. Make your own decisions and take your own risks. Let the "buck" stop when it gets to you.

The world around continues to change. Success demands that you be part of that change. Take the risks that will move you ahead. Forge ahead with new approaches and new ideas.

Whatever the imagination can picture, man can successfully accomplish. Whatever you reasonably set out to do, you will get done.

Work with what you have, no matter what the limitations. Continue to look for *how* your goals can be accomplished. If anyone can get the job done, why not you?

Look for solutions. Look for ways to turn problems into opportunities. Stimulate the imagination of those about you. Inspire them to do much more. Encourage them to be part of the total effort but make sure they participate in the rewards as well as the problems.

Above all, to make things happen, you've got to sell. Everything depends on people believing that it will be done!

14

EXECUTIVE
DECISION MAKING

An executive is characterized by the way he thinks. The important ability that distinguishes one top executive from another is the capacity to use one's head.

The ability to make decisions and use good judgment are critical factors. Choices must be made—often with little more than a hunch to go by.

To make the right decisions you need to develop an integrated sense of values. An executive must *believe*. It is not enough to have a superficial knowledge and parrot-like ability to repeat what you read or hear. You need to be a completely integrated *real* person, one who knows himself. You must integrate your entire business, social, moral, ethical, and political world. It must all fit and blend together for you. You have got to see the relationships and interrelationships. You must in essence *be yourself*.

You cannot try to imitate. Learn all you can from others but develop as a unique and individual person.

Help to provide your organization with purpose, drive, imagination, and a set of values by which sound decisions could be made. Operate in a broad frame of reference. Relate your responsibility, your organization, and your goals to the larger framework of which you are a part. If you run a department think in terms of what is best for the company. Orient your thinking to overall needs. If you run a larger group or a company think in terms of your market, the community, and society.

This kind of orientation will give you a basis for better and more consistent decisions, decisions which are easier to make. It will identify you too as a man capable of higher responsibility and one destined for growth.

How Managers Decide

Decisions usually involve a choice among alternatives. Sometimes the choice is an obvious one.

Very often, however, the matter is complex. Many factors are involved. The one best answer is not readily apparent.

Make it easy for yourself. Make frequent small decisions instead of occasional major ones. Test, reappraise, and re-evaluate as you go along. If it fits the situation, decide one step at a time.

Let us say, for example, that you have your eye on one of the juniors in your company. You think he is capable of doing more. He looks like a man who can handle a substantial share of management responsibility. He may be a salesman who impresses you as a capable Branch Manager. If at all practical, promote him in small steps. Make him a Sales Supervisor over just a few men. If he performs well and still appears to be able to handle more, promote him later to Sales Manager with responsibility over more men. If still indicated, you can make him Branch Manager after that. This is a practical example of making a series of small decisions rather than one big decision.

If a man is a clerk and you think he could run the department, make him a Section Supervisor first or a Staff Assistant. Don't overwhelm him with a lot of responsibility he has never had before. Give him the opportunity to grow into the job and give yourself the advantage of observing how he handles added responsibility before you move him all the way.

You can do an employee a disservice and hurt his future by promoting him too fast. Don't force him into making a lot of mistakes and a lot of enemies. Don't push him into losing his self-confidence.

I have seen men who were put into such positions lose confidence in themselves, become anxious and upset over the possibility of not being able to handle the job, and as a cover-up become overbearing and arbitrary with their subordinates.

Let us consider another type of situation where numerous small decisions may be preferable to infrequent but major decisions. The problem, we will presume, concerns a proposed plan to expand manufacturing facilities. Additional plant and equipment are needed to process the current backlog. Customers are demanding faster delivery, but the present facilities could not handle the requirements. There are indications that the present heavy demand will continue for some time but nobody knows for sure whether this will be so and how long this condition will last. The further you look into the future the more difficult it is to be sure of what the needs will be. If you commit for an additional 100,000 square feet of space and $2,000,000 worth of equipment and it finally turns out that the demand does not last for more than a year or so, you stand to lose a great deal. You would not get a chance to amortize the costs.

If you delay making the decision you will force customers to go elsewhere for their needs. You will help competition to grow. Stronger competition would of course hurt even more as time goes on.

On the principle of deciding a bit at a time, you might want to rent or build 20,000 square feet of space with options to add space later on. Or you may buy the land and build manufacturing facilities of only 20,000 square feet with provisions in the building plans for additions as needed.

The same would be true of equipment. Only the equipment needed immediately would be purchased. If the lead time on delivery requirements for the equipment covers a long period of time, you might commit to some additional equipment with options to take it within a specified period of time.

Decide Now; Announce Later

Another practical technique is what we call the "Decide now, announce later" method.

Leaders *must* make decisions. They *must* take action. More often than not some kind of action—even the wrong kind—is better than no action at all. Activity generates enthusiasm and enthusiasm is vital for progress.

This does not mean you should make hasty and unwise decisions. When a problem comes up you are not expected to give an answer off the top of your head. People lose confidence, in fact, in managers who seem to make hasty decisions. They like to feel the problem was important enough to merit careful consideration.

When you decide on a course of action commit only as much as you need to. Allow yourself time to adjust and maneuver.

Do not take this to mean you should put off decisions. Announce, however, only that part of the decision that needs to be announced.

Write Them Down

Carry a pad and pencil with you. Ideas are elusive. They will drift out of your grasp as readily as they drift in. Get the idea down in black and white right away. Don't let it get away from you.

In trying to find the best course among many alternatives and picking out the advantages versus the drawbacks on a proposed course of action, there are several techniques you could use.

One is the simple expediency of listing all of the advantages and disadvantages of the proposed action. You would be amazed how simple it becomes after you get it down in writing. This is a mere listing without any conscious effort to weigh one advantage against a possible drawback. While doing this you will subconsciously be weighing the relative merits of each factor anyway.

Give It Time to Hatch

This brings up another practice of making decisions. If you have the time—and you usually do—let it stew! After you have given the problem serious thought and the decision seems to be a difficult one, go on to something else. Forget about the problem for a while. Your subconscious will be sorting out the important from the irrelevant. You will unknowingly be weighing the factors. You will be more relaxed and when you get back to the problem you will see it in much better perspective. The decision will seem more obvious.

You will often find that mysteriously, while taking a walk, driving home from work, arising in the morning, or during some other period of mental relaxation, an important inspiration will come to you. What actually happens is that all the data you poured into your human computer starts to settle and sifts itself out. Let your subconscious mind take over for a while. You will often get the best answer that way.

The Weighted Factor Technique

The weighted factor technique is one which will often help with a complex problem. This is a system whereby you decide beforehand how much weight you will assign to each factor.

Let us say that you are trying to decide on the purchase of certain invoicing equipment. You have seen demonstrations of several accounting machine manufacturers and you have listened to the stories of the various salesmen. You feel that the following factors are important in considering new equipment:

1. Ability of the manufacturer's personnel to teach your people how to use the equipment, help to devise the systems and forms to be used with the equipment, and have the technical know-how to assure the efficient working of the new system.
2. Reliability of equipment and service facilities should any breakdowns occur.
3. Savings which would result from the use of specific types of equipment.
4. Initial investment and terms of payment.
5. Delivery schedule. Which machine can be delivered soonest?

Each of the factors are obviously not as significant as the others. You may decide, for instance, that factor number one (ability of the manufacturer's personnel to get the new system started) is the most important. You assign a value of 10 to factor number one.

Factor number two (reliability of equipment and service facilities) is considered of next importance and its relative value to you is 8.

Savings to your company in the long run are important to you and beyond assurance of a smooth transition and continuation of operation, you feel that factor number three is of next importance. You assign a value of 7.

While initial cost is important you feel that in the long run it will not mean too much. You therefore assign to factor number four a value of 5.

To factor number five (delivery schedule) you assign a value of 3 because here again you realize that in the long run this is not one of the most important factors. (While we are presuming so in the present hypothetical case, there could be situations of course where the need to switch to new equipment is urgent and a much higher value would be assigned to this factor.)

In trying to weigh the merits of Invoicing Machine A versus Machine B, your worksheet might look like this:

Machine A is sold by a company whose sales and technical personnel are highly trained and capable. You therefore assign 8 out of a possible 10 to factor one.

They have well organized service facilities and their equipment appears to be well engineered. You give two a rating of 7.

Conversion from the present billing system to the equipment and process represented by Machine A would result in the largest possible saving. You give to factor three the full 10 points.

The initial cost of Machine A against the other model is the highest. On factor four therefore Machine A rates poorly and you assign a rating of 1.

Manufacturer A cannot deliver and install for another six months because of a heavy backlog. To factor five you assign a low rating of 2.

Machine B's sales and technical personnel are well trained but they do not seem to attract the caliber of people which Manufacturer A does. They have fairly adequate service facilities. Their equipment is designed to result in good savings over a period of time. The initial cost is lower than that of Model A and the machine can be delivered in three months. The ratings assigned to the various factors are shown in Chart I and reflect these facts:

Chart I

FACTORS

Models	#1	#2	#3	#4	#5
A	8	7	10	3	2
B	5	7	7	6	5

We will now multiply each factor by the weighted values:

Chart II
Machine A

Factor	Rating Assigned	Weighted Value	Total Value
#1	8	10	80
#2	7	8	56
#3	10	7	70
#4	1	4	4
#5	2	3	6

Total weighted value for Machine A 216

Machine B

Factor	Rating Assigned	Weighted Value	Total Value
#1	5	10	50
#2	5	8	40
#3	7	7	49
#4	6	4	24
#5	5	3	15

Total weighted value for Machine B 178

On the basis of this kind of weighted valuation the choice would be Machine A.

In actual practice there are usually more than two models or two choices involved. We kept it as simple as we could for the illustration. On a complex problem you would go back and forth changing ratings and values as you go along. You reappraise and re-evaluate and you consider and literally *weigh* the problem, but you force yourself to put it down in precise terms. Here too the sum of small decisions leads to one big obvious and simple conclusion.

This technique helps too where you have several people involved in making the decision and general agreement seems impossible. Get agreement on specific factors and weights first.

That should be much easier. Then work out the problem together on the weighted factor technique. The final decision is easily arrived at.

Get the Facts

You will never have all the facts you would like to have before making a decision. Decision making in business involves risk taking and it is the person who takes the risks that often makes the greatest gains. The one who plays it safe ends up in mediocrity.

Be that as it may, *do* get all the facts you can before making up your mind. Don't fly by the seat of your pants only for the glory of doing so. Whenever possible, actions must be based on factual information and sound unbiased thinking.

Look for facts as they are, not as they might be or as you might wish them to be. This is very important, no matter what you want to accomplish. If you want to ignore some facts later in order to do what you somehow feel is the right thing to do, fine, but don't try to twist the facts in your own mind. Look at the facts squarely as they *are* and *know* why you are ignoring them in arriving at a course of action.

Identify the problem rather than the symptom. The office staff being irritable and uncooperative is more likely to be a symptom rather than a problem. You will never bring about an improvement unless you identify the *problem* and work on *that*. The problem in this case may be insufficient space, poor lighting, or poor supervision. The even more basic problem is poor efficiency as reflected by irritable workers and possibly caused by the crowding and poor lighting. If you work on symptoms rather than problems you will always be putting out fires. You will seldom arrive at long term solutions or improvements.

If a situation involves other people you will get at many more facts if you discuss the situation with them. If a decision is apt to affect others talk with them first before jumping to conclusions. Even if your decision is right you will have a harder time selling it to the people it affects if you haven't taken them along with you in your examination of the problem. People understand directives a lot better when they have lived through the steps that led to the directive.

In many decisions the facts cannot all be known. Even if the needed facts could be known, there may not be enough time to dig them out. Get as many facts as you can and pick out those that are most relevant and significant. Do not hesitate however to use your judgment when lack of facts or lack of time prevents thorough consideration of the problem.

As a manager of people, you will never know in detail what each of your subordinates knows about his particular specialty. Despite this, you can often help them to find answers to problems in their own fields. You can do this by knowing *how to ask questions.*

From the right questions flow the right answers. Make them think of every facet. Encourage them to look at the problem from all viewpoints. Consider all possible combinations. Question every premise and every conclusion.

Let them *teach* you the technical facts of the problem you are discussing. In the process of explaining it to you and answering some of the basic questions you will ask, the problem will become much more clear to them. There is no better way to learn something than to try to teach it.

You would be amazed how you could help the specialist or others solve problems in their own areas on matters that you yourself know little about. You can be the catalyst for helping others solve their problems.

In looking for the facts, keep looking at the big picture. Keep relating everything to everything else. Nothing stands alone. More and more you will be relying on specialists but unless you keep the entire situation before you and unless you examine the assumptions from which your specialists proceed you will have difficulty in getting the significant facts.

Use Your Judgment

It is judgment, not knowledge, which puts a man at the top.

Top executives are characterized by a desire to change things, the ability to take timely action, and the use of sound judgment.

Everyone's strong characteristic and best quality, if carried to extremes, could become a serious fault. A man who was promoted because of his enthusiasm could find that over-enthusiasm coupled with hasty actions could prevent him from doing a good job at the higher level.

A man who was advanced because of his experience, his good judgment, and ability to weigh the facts could find that over-caution results in failure at the higher position because he cannot sparkplug the kind of enthusiasm and growth his company needs.

Make sure you think it through. What does your job require? Forget about the kind of emphasis which was needed in your last job. What is needed *here?*

Do you *understand* what has to be done? Do you *listen* to what your associates are saying? Do you *know* what the problem is before you start to recommend solutions?

You must understand the role you should be playing in your position. A Treasurer can no longer play the part of the Accountant or Office Manager. A Branch Manager is no longer expected to perform as a Salesman or a Branch Sales Manager. Too many never realize that their new positions bring new responsibilities and require new outlooks.

Judgment becomes more important as you move up. You've

got to keep things moving, but you must be right most of the time. To be able to form the right judgment you have got to study all facets of your job. You must be aware of everything you might have to know. You must listen to as many well informed people as you can.

Informed and independent judgment becomes more important as you receive greater responsibility in business. Make sure you think things through.

Focus not only on the troublespots or the things that are bothering you this week. Keep looking at the bigger picture and the broader area no matter what the pressures. Unless you do this you will be unpleasantly surprised by other troublespots next week and next month.

Learn to distinguish the probable from the improbable; the possible from the impossible.

There are no specific answers to most questions in management. There is no 1-2-3 technique or steps to handle all management problems. There are no pat answers. There are no invariable yardsticks, rules-of-thumb, or ready made answers.

Management is by and large a matter of judgment, *your* judgment if you are the manager. The advertising agency doesn't really know the "right" media to use or the best copy slant; the industrial psychologist cannot give you detailed instructions on how you should handle Joe Brown; the systems specialist doesn't really have all the answers to your administrative problems. These people could help you to decide but if it's your responsibility, your judgment is as good as theirs—only better.

The principles, techniques, and policies which you are taught are guides and only guides. The appropriate answer lies in your good judgment and in that alone.

Note that I say "appropriate" answer, not "right" answer for in the dynamic field of business and management, where changes are constant, there is no one right answer or action.

Don't Pass the Buck

The story was told some years ago about two seedy looking characters who were sitting on a park bench. One looked to the other and said "I'm a guy who never took advice from anybody." "Not me, pal," said the other, "I'm a man who followed everybody's advice."

You lose either way. Get all the good advice you can, but you and you alone have the final responsibility for the decision. Nobody can make your decision for you.

This is why they say that top management is a lonely business. When the moment of decision comes you have to make the choice all by yourself.

Don't pass the buck to others. Even if you make a mistake once in a while accepting the responsibility for an occasional error will gain friends and respect for you. The ability and willingness to make decisions will result in your being consulted more and more by an increasing number of your associates. Get to be known as someone who knows how to make a decision and who isn't afraid to make it.

If you are the man with the title and the responsibility you will have to make the important decisions. You can buy people and ideas but you cannot buy decisions.

I knew of a company many years ago who called in one of the better known management consultants to examine and review its organizational, manufacturing, and marketing setup. The management consultants were given carte blanche to make the study and there was little or no significant consultation back and forth during the course of this study. At the end of several months a report was submitted to top management of this company and the company went ahead and started to put into operation every single recommendation.

It almost ruined the company!

It almost ruined the company because the management shirked its decision-making responsibility. It thought it could turn it over to the consultants whose job it was to give advice but who were not responsible for making the final decisions. This kind of thing happens every day in business. Get all the advice you can, but don't pass the buck when it comes to making the decisions. Be big enough to make all of *your* decisions *yourself.*

Don't however hog the decisions that should be made down the line. Decision making is vastly improved if as a manager you would make fewer (but more important) decisions. Many decisions could be made by others in your organization and they should be *required* to make them. Don't let your subordinates pass their decision responsibility up to you—and more important, don't pass *your* decision responsibility up to your boss. Decisions should be made at the lowest possible levels and as close to the scene of action as possible.

Forcing your subordinates to make their own decisions is sometimes difficult. Some of the decisions won't be the same as the ones you would make. You will learn however to sit back and watch your people make a few mistakes of their own. They will learn a lot more that way.

Nothing Can Override Your Own Mind

Woodrow Wilson once said "One cool judgment is worth a thousand counsels."

The quality of your decisions will determine the reputation you will build as a business executive and will determine the responsibility and leadership challenges you will assume.

After all is said and done, after you have used every single technique you know of in decision making, after you have talked with some of the finest minds concerning the problem, there is one principle that should guide you in *all* decision making, in business or in private life! *Nothing must override your own mind.*

Place absolutely nothing above the verdict of your own mind. Everything must be consistent to *you.* You and you alone are responsible for your decisions, not your associates and not your superiors. They could suggest or they could decide for themselves, but they could never decide for you. You alone are responsible for your decisions and your actions.

If you announce it as your decision, if you sign your name to it, if it is supposed to come from you, make sure it is *yours.*

Encourage New Thinking

"Brainstorming" is a way to increase your idea power and creative output. This is a free-association technique. Whenever you can, for instance, allow time for unrestricted expression.

In brainstorming a positive attitude is established. It usually works best in smaller groups consisting of people in like job status. Any idea which anyone thinks of is thrown in, no matter how slightly relevant it may be. Others add to or build on that idea. No criticism or evaluation is permitted during the brainstorming session. All you want to do is to get new ideas in a completely uninhibited atmosphere. Evaluation could come at a later time.

Even the most outlandish idea could lead to a valuable creation. Brainstorming could generate completely new thinking and will suggest new approaches to old problems.

The elimination of judgment from the idea creation stage is one of the most powerful reasons this technique works. Since no evaluation is allowed a climate is created in which each member feels free to express ideas they may otherwise hesitate to reveal. People are encouraged to suggest unusual ideas and to break away from traditional approaches to problems.

The principle involved in brainstorming is just as effective in talking to one subordinate or one associate in the normal course of business. If they are making a suggestion don't be quick to evaluate or criticize. Don't kill the idea before it has a chance to even make an appearance.

Another variation of brainstorming which I have found most effective is to sometimes tell an associate half the story or proposed plan. Let him jump to conclusions as to what the idea is which you are about to describe. Because his viewpoint and experience is *always* different from yours the conclusion he jumps to or the idea he fills in will often be different from what you were going to say—and will sometimes lead you to a more productive thought.

Ideas can explode. The power of creative ideas is beyond measurement. New ideas however work best when they occur within the framework of an organized system. Encourage those about you to develop and suggest new approaches. Encourage them to look at opportunities from new viewpoints.

Approve new ideas as far as you can, even though you are not sure they will work. It will often lead to other ideas and will encourage your people to continue to look for better ways to get things done.

Decisions That Make Things Happen

Plans, discussions, committee reports, and deliberations are worthless unless decisions are made and *action* taken. Positive action is sometimes difficult to get.

People often need a push to get over the basic inertia that prevents action. They are inclined to let things stand. The status quo is comfortable.

See that complacency does not take hold. Probe and search for ways to improve your competitive position. Continue to take action to adjust to a changing environment and in fact adjust in such a way that you take advantage of the changing environment.

The fact that most people are content with the status quo and will not make changes until the problem is squarely and irreparably before them provides you with one of the best opportunities in management. Look ahead to what the situation is likely to be. Think ahead to what people will want and need . . . and take action as you go along!

Plan for action. The lack of action could usually be traced to the absence of a plan for action.

What do you do however if you are the type of person who makes many plans and has every good intention of carrying out those plans, but never seems to get around to it? Here's a trick that could work wonders for you. *Write it down*. Make a note of everything you plan to do.

These notes could be on small scraps of paper. The important thing is to write it down. Don't cross it off the list until you have taken the action or decided against taking the action. Know why you have changed your mind and never permit "I'll do it in a few days" to influence you. That note or scrap of paper will hound you until you take the action. It won't let you "conveniently" forget.

This technique too will get you away from making vague plans you never intended to carry out. If it is important you will write it down. If you write it down, you will do it.

Try it. You will see how much more you accomplish that way.

You Can't Wait Forever

Another serious roadblock to effective executive action is the tendency to look for perfection. A successful executive cannot be a perfectionist. This is so important that I would like to put it into even stronger terms. *A perfectionist can never be a successful business executive.*

You will never have complete facts and the situation will never be just right for action. You will always be faced with alternatives, the result of which you could never be sure of.

Do the best you can under the circumstances. Get as many facts as you can with no more time and effort than the problem is entitled to. Make your decision, take your action, and go on to the next thing. If you wait for all you think you need, if you insist upon perfection, you will never get anything accomplished.

The environment in which we live is always changing. It is not possible to get definitive answers about social or business sciences while we are going through the time period under study. We will never know how the economy really is today until we have passed through the period and can look back. Those who say "let's wait to see what happens" find that nothing ever happens—to them. Nothing good, at least!

We will never know whether sales are picking up right now. We will know that they picked up over the past few weeks. We will know what is happening today a few weeks from now. *Today* however we have to make decisions on what we *think* will happen. We have to make decisions and take action on incomplete facts and in imperfect situations. Wisdom, experience, decision, and action are needed. Perfection is not an attribute here. Good management is in many ways the application of common sense to business problems. This perhaps is most important of all.

Let Your Intuition Doublecheck Your Logic

After all is said and done, after you have examined all the facts, you think you know the situation fairly well. You have used the various decision making techniques. You can't rule out your intuition.

"Flying by the seat of your pants" sometimes has merit even in today's more sophisticated management world. Having gone through all the scientific steps, all the data, factors, and alternatives are stored in your mind, as facts are in an electronic computer. What you regard as a hunch is often the result of a digesting of the facts by your human computer.

If after all your consideration you feel strongly that a particular course of action is the way you should go, even though it does not *seem* to be a logical outcome of the thinking process you just went through, follow your convictions. You will find in the long run that what you might call intuition is a pretty powerful way for your convictions to come to bear.

Delay the Impulse

You are expected to give serious consideration to what comes to your attention. You will find for instance that you cannot always joke with subordinates. What you may treat lightly, they may regard as quite serious because they are always looking to you for hints of what may happen next.

If you are the boss you are a very important person. You are a key manager in a critical spot. Make sure you act the part. Don't move on first impulse. Don't take forever to answer questions, but:

Review your thoughts before you voice them; do not snap answers, questions or comments at people.

Take the words or needs of others seriously, even when you must contradict or deny them.

Announce your decisions seriously and carefully.

Appear judicious. Create the image of a fair, truthful, and skilled manager. When you put things off appear to be doing so for good reasons.

Resist the temptation to jump at the first solution that comes along. There are other possible alternatives. Withhold decisions until you have heard all the arguments. Just as men want the dignity of the law to settle their legal cases, employees want the dignity of a mature executive to settle their managerial affairs.

Don't act on impulse. Wait before you act, even if for only a second or two. Cultivate the style of a calm, steady, and judicial executive.

Decide and Move On

Don't waste time making unproductive decisions. Define the problem. Distinguish the important from the unimportant. Don't come back to the same problem long after it should have been taken care of.

Be sure you really identify the problem. You may be working on one isolated part of the problem whereas in fact the real problem covers a much broader area and the broader area must be solved first.

Suppose for instance that you are looking for ways to cut costs of printing business forms which your company sells. If you devote your full attention to this phase of the situation you may fail to see its proper relationship or forget why cutting costs seems to be important. The real problem may be declining sales. You have to find the *causes* of the problem first. If the cause is inability on the part of your sales force to locate the right prospects or inability of your plant to meet delivery requirements, why devote your efforts to cutting costs? That is not your problem. You may in fact be aggravating the situation by cutting costs as that may further hamper your ability to improve deliveries or improve salesmen training.

Solve the problem once. Make your decision only once. The job then is to follow through to effective action!

Select the Input

The people you listen to will have a great deal to do with the quality of your decisions and effectiveness of your actions. Listen to those whose thinking is sharper. Harness the best brain power you can get access to. Surround yourself with those who will argue constructively and force you to sharpen your judgment.

Seek out those who exercise positive influences. Forget those who insist on going by the book in preference to being resourceful and imaginative.

Avoid the neutralists or the eternal philosophers. They will only waste your time telling you how things used to be or just shooting the breeze.

Perspective is essential. Communicate with people having different interests and different viewpoints.

Create Them and Sell Them

The more people you get to participate in the problem, the more likely you are to come up with good answers.

Build your idea source. Go to conventions, travel, visit other plants, lunch with creative people, scan all kinds of magazines.

Sell your ideas. Figure out the benefits. Think about the people who will help you install the idea, those who will work with it. Win support by showing them they will gain from it. Give as many people credit as you can.

In a Nutshell

It is judgment, not knowledge, which puts a man at the top.

It is often wiser to make frequent smaller decisions than to let things stagnate until major decisions or major changes are necessary. Where appropriate, announce only those parts of the decision that need to be known and reserve the flexibility to change the rest of the plan to meet changing needs. Commit ideas and plans to writing as quickly as you can.

If the problem is complex, don't force the solution. Giving ideas time to hatch will often encourage the right solutions to develop. The weighted factor technique works well where the problem is complex or where approval of many is required.

Gather all the facts you can before making a decision but remember that a perfectionist cannot succeed in business. You will never have, beforehand, all the facts you would like to have. A business leader learns to move ahead with what he has.

Above all, be yourself. All you do must be consistent to you. Nothing must be permitted to override your own mind. Never act against your own better judgment.

Cultivate sources for creative thinking. Sell the ideas you create and encourage others to create. Make decisions and get things done.

15

WHAT TO DO
WHEN YOU GET
THE BALL

What are the things you ought to be thinking about and paying attention to when you step into a new job? What techniques and principles will assure that when you do get the responsibility you turn it into one of the greatest opportunities of your life.

The first thing you should remember upon your assignment to your first management job or to your first big job is to be yourself. You were selected because of what you are, what you have done, and what you can do. Don't try to change your personality by becoming overbearing, and don't take the opposite approach and try to become one of the boys by being meek, subservient, and ultra-suggestible. Be yourself. Meet your problems squarely and honestly. Help where you can and accept help when it is given.

Think and act as if it were your own business. This is the foremost principle which you should follow throughout your business career. Your scope will be broader, your contributions more significant, and your growth more rewarding.

Be yourself in your dealings with your new associates and

your new superiors. It may take a little while before you are really accepted. You will be on trial at first. Your subordinates will wait to see if you know what you are talking about, if you are capable, if you can help them and if you are the kind of leader they want to follow. They will look for signs to show whether you are a regular guy and will back them up or are so insecure and unsure that you are not likely to remain in the job very long. They will test you to see if you mean what you say.

Be yourself and you will come out all right. Don't try to change everything overnight or make changes just for the sake of making changes. Know why something is done the way it is done before you change it. Listen more and talk less while you are looking around and appraising your new situation.

When you are sure, however, and when you know a change has to be made, make it and stick to it. Show that you are willing to listen at any time but will stick to your convictions until given a good reason to change them.

Your associates will be watching you too. They want to know what kind of person you are. They want to know how capable you are. They may not accept you right away, because they do have their own luncheon habits and personal business relations, but be yourself and you will be accepted. You will soon find your new position, your new surroundings, and your new relationships as pleasant and as comfortable as the ones you just left.

If it's a new company for you, incidentally, and its stock is publicly traded, one of the first things you do is to buy some of that stock. It will help you to see your company from an added dimension and will motivate you to relate your efforts to the overall objectives.

On Being Promoted

So you have been promoted? You were probably selected over several others. People who were formerly your associates or perhaps your buddies are now your subordinates. Some of them may have been disappointed. Some of them probably thought *they* deserved the promotion even more than you did.

What do you do? Do you gloat over your victory? Do you decide to show them who is boss? Do you start to crack the whip?

What you do here, the way you handle your former associates, the way you personally react to the promotion, will determine whether you will get any *more* promotions. It will determine whether you will keep going up the ladder—or will be pushed to the ground.

It is important to repeat that rule number one, two, and three is to BE YOURSELF. You were promoted for what they thought you were. Don't change.

Help the ones who were passed over. Show that you at least understand how they feel. Determine to handle your new assignment so well that it will turn out to be a good thing for those associates. Help them to grow too. Build the organization so that they have better opportunities. Help them to help you to help them get what each wants.

Help to soften the blow for the disappointed because it is the right thing to do and because you will need their cooperation. Build *that* instead of their envy and resentment.

Don't lose your humility and sympathy as you go up the ladder. Remember that what motivates your subordinates now is often what used to motivate you.

Don't take your success too seriously. What you really got was greater responsibility and the opportunities to help others in return for more money and greater job satisfaction. If you were looking for power from the promotion you will be disappointed. Modern management has changed tremendously. The iron handed autocrat cannot survive in a modern corporation where teamwork and leadership is needed. Effective management rests in a large measure on the consent of those whom you manage.

Nobody wants to work for a boss who is overly impressed with his own importance. Nobody likes a guy who tries to assert his importance or pretend his superiority by barking out orders and belittling the ability of others.

It helps to remember that all people who work for your organization, no matter what their level of business skill or job classification, are very important to some people and are superior in some skills and activities. Many talented, intelligent, and capable people do not get far in business because their interests and abilities lie in other areas. This does not make them any less important as people.

Chances are that each man who works for you excels in some area. He may be a good musician, an amateur historian, an athlete, a leader in community affairs, or a wonderful husband and father. Appreciate these abilities. You will get a lot more out of your people when you do.

We must not assume that business ability is the most important talent in the world and that those who do not excel in this area are of less importance. You could not make a more serious management error.

As success comes to you, therefore, keep your feet on the ground. Let your success be the means through which others can climb too. Be yourself all the way. Success is something that if you cannot take it in stride, you will not have.

Analyze Before You Leap

Don't make a million changes the minute you step into the new job. The mere fact that a new man is in the job is enough change in itself. Find out what it's all about before you start reorganizing everything and everyone.

The first questions you must answer, and this is not as simple as it sounds, are:

What are we in business for? What kind of business is it? What are the unique strengths and advantages? Is it a manufacturing business? Is it one which depends on its marketing force primarily? Is the raising of capital one of its principal problems? Does it have an old management or a young management? What kind of a job really needs to be done? What is the state of the department, division, or company you have just taken over? What are its customers?

The last question is perhaps the most important one of all. It is the customers, present and potential, and what they will expect from your company, that will determine the character and personality of your company.

Ask questions. Here, if any place in business, is the time to be a good listener. Appraise your people. For a manager, ability to *recognize* ability is vital.

Look at the actual lines of authority and channels of communication as well as the official ones—the formal written ones as well as the informal channels. Who really makes the decisions? Who provides the leadership? Who do people look to for decisions and direction? What do others seem to expect of you in your new position. How do you see your role?

An understanding of all of this could help you to communicate and accomplish objectives and it could help you to find your principal assistants.

Re-examine all procedures. Don't follow them blindly. Chances are that many procedures started by your predecessors, or predecessor's predecessors, have long ceased to fill a need. Don't take what's happened or what's happening for granted.

Get Around

You can't see what's going on from behind your desk. Sit in your office and you will learn only what your people want you to learn. You must get out and you must get around.

The world is becoming a lot smaller. With improvements in communication and transportation one's business, if the company is of any size at all, is no longer local. It is regional, national, and world-wide.

If your area of responsibility includes offices, plants, distributors, employees, or others in dispersed areas, you must get around to see them. It is the only way to know what is going on and the only way to provide real leadership. Travel is a required part of business life. Get used to the fact that you will be doing more and more of it.

Travel offers other opportunities too. It gives you a chance to see your business and your job from different viewpoints. Getting away from the office puts the major problems in real perspective. The trees aren't hidden for the forest.

Win Them Over

What you do during the first few weeks in the new job will determine whether your associates and your subordinates will pitch in to help, will stand disinterestedly by, or will actually try to torpedo your efforts.

Business activity is so much a group performance that a sincere interest in others will help to make you a top manager. It will permit you to lead without appearing to lead.

In leading a group, remember that each member, like yourself, is influenced by personal factors. Each has a different idea of what your relation should be as regards himself. The better you understand these factors, the more accurately you will determine what you can do to make yours an effective group.

Consider your relationships with others. Your boss, your associates, your subordinates, your business friends, or your customers. How do you affect them and why? How do they react to you, and why?

To change others you often have to change *yourself*. You will notice that some people always seem to meet friendly and co-

operative persons, while others always are confronted by un-
friendly and stubborn people.

How do you affect people? If your complaint is that "they
don't listen" to what you tell them, chances are *you* don't tell
them in the most effective way.

Encourage and inspire those about you. Many do not work
at full capacity. Many subconsciously or otherwise place a limit
in their own minds to what they want to earn. With people
that could handle more it is essential that you give them enough
to keep them stimulated. It is often wise to give a new man just
a few tasks at the start but to keep increasing his responsibilities as he demonstrates his ability to handle it. Help him to
develop at the pace which he is capable of maintaining.

Unless you stimulate others you will find they will stretch out
unimportant work and never accomplish for you or for themselves the really great things most people *can* accomplish.

Help others to advance. A man with ability will advance even
if you do not help him. You might as well be on his team. Develop, train, and promote the men under and around you. They
will get there anyway.

Some men will go up more quickly than you, others more
slowly. Help them all. Help each to go at his own pace. The
men you develop will in the long run be the measure of your
worth to top management.

If there are problems in your organization make an honest
effort to find out what they are. Employees will intuitively know
if you really want to hear what is wrong. Don't be quick to
defend or attack anything which they bring to your attention.

Don't suppress symptoms—find causes. Don't stifle it. Let it
come out.

Watch the Pendulum

Don't blow hot and cold or go from one extreme to the other.
Don't keep changing signals by the hour.

A man's greatest strength, if carried to extremes, becomes his greatest liability. A good manager is a balanced individual. An enthusiastic person could have enthusiasm become his worst characteristic if it overshadows everything else and if it subordinates wisdom and common sense. A manager who is noted for his judgment, on the other hand, could have that become his worst trait if all he does is think and never makes a move. I have even seen cases where extreme brightness held a man back from doing a good management job because with it went contempt for other people who were not so naturally endowed.

Watch the extremes. They could get you into trouble.

Don't Be a "Therewillbeno"

Look for things that *can* be done and for better ways to do them. Look for ways to accomplish things rather than for reasons why they cannot be done.

The way you *say* things, announce decisions, or issue instructions can do much to set the climate for how people will think and act. There are many ways to say "no." The smart manager could make it sound pretty much like "yes."

One Navy Captain might say *"there will be no* liberty until the ship is all cleaned up" while the Captain who knows how to whip up enthusiasm would say "all sailors may go on liberty immediately after the ship is cleaned." The second Captain gets more done—and has a happier crew.

Some managers will write "there will be no more than two weeks' vacation allowed during each year of employment" while the smart manager writes "up to two weeks of vacation will be authorized during each year of employment." The attitude between one way of saying it and the other is a lot different. The man who says it in a positive way has a happier crew, gets more done, and encourages more positive kind of thinking throughout.

A smart executive knows how to develop pride in a job well done.

The Rules of the Game

Find out as early as you can what the bases for judgment are. How will your bosses measure your work? How do they expect you to work? Are they the kind that want people to juggle fifty balls at a time or do they expect you methodically to handle one at a time?

You won't change your own way of working or your philosophy of management because of the outward measures of accomplishment which your bosses use, but you *will* slant your *apparent* or outward way of working. If they like fifty-ball jugglers but you believe that one can handle only one ball at a time and do it effectively, then create as much of an image as you can of a fifty-ball juggler but perform as a one-ball-at-a-time star.

One thing is sure, and that is that *profits* and how you contribute to them are included in the rules of the game. In business it is profits which most accurately tell how much is being accomplished. Profits to business are what boxscores are to sports. You can't tell how well the team is doing until you see the score or the figures.

There is one big difference between the company that is making money and the one that is just trodding along. The successful organization *believes* it is offering an advantage to its customers which is worth every dollar it costs. Its management believes it is giving the customer more value than the customer is paying for.

The successful company is able to say to its customers: "Our company makes a good product, fairly priced. We ask an honest price. The product or service has real value for you. The quality of the product, the type of service, and the reliability which we offer cannot be matched anywhere at this price. Anyone who is asking for less is offering less in return."

Continuously test all parts for their contribution to profits. All parts must stand on their own. Each part must justify itself. The rules of the game demand that no matter what your job is or how far it may *seem* to be related from the profit objectives, you *must* make a positive contribution to profits.

The rules of the game, or the way you will be judged, may include performance against quota or budget. They may include the ability to attract and develop people. They may concern themselves with rate of turnover.

There are usually several points on which you are being judged. Know what they are.

Know too, that the rules keep changing. The emphasis keeps changing. Don't be caught flat footed following yesterday's rules when today's are so different.

One more thought with regard to rules. If you want to do something, and it seems the right thing to do but you are not sure you're allowed to do it, you don't know what the rules really are as they pertain to what you want to do—go ahead and do it. If you don't know the rules which govern the action, chances are nobody else does. Go ahead—you will get more done and perhaps set some precedents while you do it.

The Mystery of Accounting

No matter what your specialty may be, there is one you must know something about if you are to succeed in business, and that is *accounting*. A business man not knowing something about accounting is like a baseball player not knowing how to keep score. Accounting is the system for keeping score in business.

Accountants have a language of their own. They have a premise of their own and a logic of their own. Accounting principles guide and control the large organization because it is the best known way to keep tabs on what is happening.

Tax and other government requirements assure the continuing importance of this profession.

The premises on which accounting statistics are based are sometimes arbitrary. If you let it, it can become the tail that wags the dog. If you don't understand it, you could be working for the "system" rather than the goals.

Learn something about accounting and financial control. Learn to understand what they do. Learn to use some of their excellent techniques and systems.

Learn accounting or you will be at its mercy!

You can't play the game unless you know the rules and can keep score. You will be judged by that score and cannot afford to put all your reliance on the objectivity of the scorekeeper or *his* understanding of what the rules should be for your operation.

Accounting is an inexact science. It can no more measure true profit than it can measure exact morale. You've got to know what the assumptions are under which "profit" is being measured. Accounting enlists the aid of mathematics in preparing budgets, standard costs, financial ratios, and other useful management concepts. "Inventory," "current assets," "operating ratios," and other concepts can be helpful in your management operations, but learn the rules of how they are arrived at, how they are used, and what they really mean.

Let Them In on It

One additional word on what to do when you step into the new job. No matter how it was handled before you got there, make it a point to let your associates and your subordinates know what is going on. Let them see as many of the reports as is necessary for a better understanding of their own jobs and a better feedback to them of how they are doing. Tell them as much as you can. Everyone wants to feel as if he is an important part of the organization.

Create a team effort and a team atmosphere when you step into the new job. You will make some mistakes but so what? A good manager never belabors himself for what went on before. He is always looking ahead to what is going to go on in the future.

Step *into* the job. Resolve that when you leave it you will leave a lot more than you inherited. Forget yourself, get down to work, and enjoy yourself.

In a Nutshell

You were promoted for what you are. Stay that way. Use your new position to give real leadership to those about you. Build a positive team with a will-do approach. Don't make a million changes until you know what it's all about.

Get to know the rules. What are you likely to be judged on? What's most important to your company and your job?

If you've been promoted, you've got the ball. Don't fumble it!

16

BE A PRO!

You can be a dynamic life giving influence in your business. Get more out of people. Turn what would otherwise be just equipment and facilities into production results and achievements. By mastering a few extra techniques and rising above the average you can pull yourself far ahead of your contemporaries.

Get to the Top

You've got to deal with people to get things done. This means you have to talk with them. You have to consult them. You may have some questions you need answers to.

Whom do you call? Whom do you go to? Do you talk to the stock clerk, the department manager, or the president? Do you talk to the dispatcher or the boss? Will the order clerk give you what you want or are you better off with the sales manager?

Go as high as you can and still be talking with the man who could give you the answers. Talk to the man who has the broader view, the one who knows how to get results, and the one who is not concerned with unimportant details. Go as high as you dare to and you will accomplish a lot more.

People at the top are easier to talk to. They understand more. They have more time, and they are above pettiness and triteness.

The first time I realized this was shortly after I received my Second Lieutenant bars in the Army and was sent to the China-Burma-India area. When I reported to my first station I was told that the Commanding General would see me in a few minutes. I had till then dealt with a few Captains and Majors and found them difficult enough. How was I going to get through an interview with a General?

I wasn't in the General's office sixty seconds when I felt completely relaxed. Here was a man who was easy to talk with. He seemed to be at peace somehow. He seemed to be concerned with important things and important ideas, not with details and personalities. He didn't seem impelled to impress me with his importance (and he certainly didn't have to try).

I realized then and there that once a man gets above the crowd and above the petty competition he is a lot easier to talk to and to deal with (especially if you don't represent competition to him).

It's smarter to go to the top!

The Will to Win

You will never be a champion unless you are willing to fight when the chips are down. Whether it is sports, politics, or business, a champion is one who doesn't know the meaning of the word defeat. He will stop at nothing short of success. There will be times when the odds are against you, when the going seems the toughest. This is the time to fight, fight, fight, all the way.

Learn to feel a contagious sense of excitement in what you do. Learn to get angry and to come to a boil when what you know is right has to be seen through.

Accept the premise that nothing happens unless you *make* it happen. It won't all come the easy way. When the results are worth it, fight it through to success. The risks may be high, but they are worth it if the stakes are high too.

Watch the Eye Level

This may seem like a small thing but it could mean the difference between getting what you want and setting up an invisible barrier between you and the one you want to influence. *Eye Level!* Talk eye to eye. If the other fellow is standing, you'll get through to him a lot easier if you stand too. If he is sitting, both of you would be more comfortable and receptive to each other if you sit down too.

If you think about it, you will realize how annoying it can be for someone to stand right over you at close range and talk to you while you are seated. It makes the man seem overbearing.

A pro watches things like eye level. He knows how to make a friend of the other fellow. He knows that friendliness begets friendliness. He knows that people he feels friendly to will react in a friendly way to him.

It is just as easy to make the other fellow comfortable and to make him feel receptive—and it's more effective too.

Go for 125 Percent

In order to accomplish what you have set out to do, you have to work on *more* than what you hope to accomplish. A certain percentage of what you plan for and work on will not turn out successfully. Let us say that eighty percent of what you work on turns out as you wanted it—and that is a pretty good average. If you want to accomplish 100 percent (and that is only par) you have to work on accomplishing 125 percent of objectives. If you attain 80 percent of that you will at least attain 100 percent of what you really wanted to get done in the first place. (80 percent of 125 percent is 100 percent.)

Keep It in Gear

To be successful you must have the ability to maintain a high level of thrust. You have to keep going toward the objective every moment of the time. Though you may do it quietly, you have to drive, drive, drive, toward your goals. Maintain an outward aura of calm, but keep up an unrelenting drive.

The kind of drive you need is the ability to *conclude* what you start. It is the ability to see things through to a finish. It is a drive which consists not of mere motions, but of *results*.

Don't mistake motion and words for positive action and accomplishments. Time spent on problems is useless unless it is pinpointed and directed to accomplishment. Don't panic subordinates by fast and furious instructions, orders, and memos, and expect results as a consequence. Planning ahead and keeping up a steady pace—keeping the action in gear—avoids the need for hasty movements.

As you get promoted and assigned from one job to the other, in what may be an attempt to prepare or train you for even higher management, do not lose sight of the fact that a job must be done at each step of the way. Learn to accomplish objectives as you go along.

Even if you believe your present assignment is a short one and will last only until you are given the next job in the training or promotion program, take advantage of the opportunity to learn all you can. Get in the habit of producing *results*. Don't play to the gallery or just hope to come up with one or two bright ideas while you are there. Even though you may have your eye on the job ahead, perform in the one you are now assigned. That's the surest way to keep going ahead.

I have seen men throw away success opportunities because they never learned to produce and accomplish at each stage.

You might move more quickly for a while but it will be a quicksand type of growth. You will overextend yourself and fall flat on your face before you get to the top.

You owe it to yourself and your boss to turn in a full and honest job every step of the way.

Plan Boldly and Act Cautiously

Here is a philosophy of management that could lead you to the top.

Plans should include every possible contingency, as wild as they may seem. Plans should be made for as far ahead into the future as the imagination will permit. The further into the future, the less need there is for "practicality." You would be amazed at how practical the ideas will become once they are developed and refined.

Allow no inhibitions to slow you down in your planning. Be as daring as possible. *Think Big* really applies here. Plan from all possible angles. Tradition, policy, or present practice has no place in future planning. The further you plan and the more frequently you revise your plans, the more certain you will be that present every-day actions and every-day decisions will be more fruitful. You will find less that has to be undone or changed. You will experience more progress from less activity.

Whether you do it formally or not is of no importance. The plan boldly—act cautiously philosophy applies to personal as well as business life.

Everyone should have at least a five-year plan. Plans for the first year should be specific and practical. Projections should spell out details and measurable objectives. The plan should be revised and re-evaluated as often as necessary.

Plans for the second year should be in outline form and include broader objectives. The second-year plan should include an element of imagination and dream.

Plans for the third, fourth, and fifth years should have successively less practicality and more imagination. The fifth year projection would include goals which are as creative and imaginative as you can possibly make them. They should be set to standards that are *way* above present accomplishments.

The second part of this philosophy states "Act cautiously." Is this consistent?

It certainly is.

Check every possibility before making a commitment. Be as sure as you can be before rendering a decision. Don't be afraid of being over-conservative. You can't be over-conservative if your forward planning has been bold.

The present action, which you may feel is conservative and about which you have so much confidence, seems conservative only in the framework of bold forward planning. You will find that you are progressing faster than others and that each step is a sure step toward the longer range plan. Conversely you will find that no matter how boldly you plan five years ahead, when you get there what you thought was bold and presumptuous turns out to be just a little bit ahead of competition.

Make It Pay

You will find your time extremely limited. Time will be one of the most important assets you have. It has to be invested wisely.

Apply the concept of "maximum return on investment" in everything you do. Spend your time where it will bring the greatest results. Spend your money where you will get more in return. Assign your people where the return on investment will be greatest. Make everything you do pay well. Follow this concept and you will be a hard man to keep down.

Don't Overmanage

Executives are often inclined to do *more* than they should rather than less. The kind of manager that seems to go from one crises to the other and follows a sort of "management by crises" pattern isn't likely to accomplish much (except maybe get ulcers or give them to him associates).

Don't blow hot and cold. Plan ahead. Avoid wide swings in the pendulum.

Don't decide, for instance, to put all emphasis on selling product Y this week, or all emphasis on cost saving, or on hiring people. Adjust to the problems, yes, but do a balanced job of managing.

Don't be one of those fellows who is always shifting his feet from the accelerator to the brake and back to the accelerator. A little headway enables you to drive more smoothly and to be surer of getting to your destination.

There Is Lots of Room for the Individualist

You will hear a lot about how corporations want the conformists and that the individualists have no place in business. Don't let them mislead you. The man with character, imagination, ability, and a mind of his own is the *only* kind who will rise to the top. He does have to be a team player and he does have to observe the courtesies and good tastes of group activity, but *to get to the top he must be an individualist.*

The out and out individualist has in fact displaced the so-called organization man in many corporations whose problem it is to explore and forge ahead in relatively untried fields (and that is often where there is the greatest growth.)

A paradox has in fact been developing in the use of psychologically examining applicants for management assignment. More and more tests and professional screening services are being used, but less and less reliance is being placed on any one test or report.

This is a good trend. It is important to know as much as possible the characteristics, the qualities, the strengths, and the weaknesses of management candidates. The selection, however, is made not on the basis of having him fit a pre-determined pattern or mold, but on the basis of finding the best man for the job—the man who will get the job done!

There is plenty of room for the bold individual who is willing to be set apart from the herd. Industry needs men of originality with the courage to approach problems from fresh standpoints. The executive whose major aim is to do his company's bidding may be all right for middle management, but he will never do for the top job.

Field managers in fact are experiencing a change in corporate thinking. More and more they are being brought in to headquarters meetings, not to be told exactly what to do, but to play an increasing role in arriving at basic decisions and courses of action.

Remember, however, that one must conform to the courtesies and etiquette of business and must be a team player. Brash and overt individualism for the sole purpose of seeming different is stupid. The winner is the man who thinks as an individual and behaves as a group member.

Make Sure the Meetings Help

There's one thing you can be sure of. If you are in management you will be involved with meetings. How well you handle the meetings, handle yourself in the meetings, and use meetings, will have a lot to do with how well you succeed in your job.

Meetings can be a help or a hindrance. Whether they turn out to be one or the other will depend on why you have them (if you are the one who is calling them) and how you run them. Don't let it be said that any committee or meeting in which *you* have a responsible part is a group of the unfit, appointed by the unwilling, to do the unnecessary. Too many meetings or committees are just that. *Use meetings to get results.*

Let's look at it first from the point of view of you as the manager calling the meeting. Make sure it is a *productive* conference. In leading a conference avoid stifling the discussion when you disagree with a statement. *Guide* the meeting. Don't smother it. Let the other points of view come out. The other fellow may have something important to say, though it may take him a little longer to get it out. Let the others talk just as much as your timing permits. If the meeting is for the purpose of exchanging views and arriving at group decisions, make sure the group participates.

If the others in the group are important to carrying out whatever decisions are arrived at at the meeting, make sure they have a major voice in determining what is to be done and how it should be done. You can learn a lot from other people.

Don't let it get out of hand, however. There *is* a time limit to business meetings. They can't be permitted to go on forever (and some people in the group may try to do just that if you let them). When progress slows down, when you reach a point of diminishing returns, or when you feel a subject has been sufficiently discussed, go on to another topic. Keep it moving. You want them to talk, but you want them to talk only for the purpose of *accomplishing* things. Keep the meeting going, getting maximum return on the investment of everybody's time.

You will sometimes be faced with the opposite problem— getting people to talk. This often happens at the beginning of a conference. Nobody wants to start. Try the "full minute of silence" technique. It will seem like eternity but be assured that someone will speak to break the silence. Asking questions of specific people will often start the ball rolling.

Meetings are potentially a most effective aid to real communication.

Never plan "to hold a meeting." If that is what you are doing, it is likely to turn out to be a waste of time. Meetings are one way of getting things done or getting problems solved. If you are planning to solve a problem by holding a meeting, that is fine. Don't plan meetings, however, and then decide what you are going to cover in the meeting. Use the meeting as the tool, not the end.

Have as few people as you can to the meeting and still accomplish your purpose. Use care in selecting who will attend. Only those who can contribute, or who can effectively learn, should be invited to a meeting. Additional people will slow down progress.

Become known as an on-timer. Start your meetings on time. Don't tolerate lateness, even if you do it in a nice way. (An effective way, very often, is to stop your meeting when the latecomer arrives, pause a moment or two, and say cheerfully, "Good morning, Jim." He'll get the message and so will everyone else.)

Once you become known as an on-timer, you will find people coming to future meetings promptly. They will learn that you will not permit the latecomers to waste the time of those who get there when they should.

Follow through after the meeting. You could *decide* things at meetings but you can't really *do* very much. Unless there is effective follow-through, the meeting will again have turned out to be a waste of time.

Meetings can be the forum for creating new ideas, new approaches, and new solutions. In a meeting of this kind encourage the lively clash of ideas, exchange of opinion, and exploration of new routes of action.

When you go to a meeting, it is often wise to keep notes. Summarize from time to time. It will often enable *you* to control the group—to be the real leader—even if someone else may be acting as the chairman. There are times when this is desirable.

The one who summarizes from time to time is often able to exert more influence on the group, especially when *no* chairman has been designated. This will happen in an impromptu kind of meeting.

Where you sit at a meeting could be important. Unless you are assigned to a place, don't just take any place. Sit where you can be seen and where you can see the expressions on the others' faces. Expressions could give you a lot of "feedback" to guide you in your efforts to accomplish what you want to accomplish at the meetings. It will help you to understand what the others are really saying. Don't sit in the back row. If you were invited to take part in a conference, *take* part in it.

If two of you are going into a relatively small meeting and you want to sell others on a point of view, don't sit together. Don't set up a "they" against "you" stage. Make it seem like a discussion back and forth. At least one of you should sit with them so that they could more easily identify themselves with your point of view.

There are many subtle things that enter into deciding where you want to sit. Look around. Give it some thought. Wherever possible, *you* decide where to sit and know why you decided to sit there. Don't leave it to chance.

If you are running the meeting, don't hand out material and talk while they are expected to read it. Give *them* the same chance you had to read it before talking. If they're supposed to read it before you speak, distribute it before the meeting or stop while they read it.

Unless it's intended as a speech or a lecture, make your meetings audience centered and not speaker centered. The speaker centered meeting may go more quickly and more smoothly, but it won't accomplish as much.

A meeting without some dissent fails to reach its full potential. A complete lack of disagreement is not good. If the meeting goes too smoothly it may be a sign of insufficient interest or an indication that the people fear to speak frankly.

If you are the chairman, stimulate discussion. Encourage the members to function as a team, but don't do their thinking for them. Raise questions. Encourage the shy ones to speak more and keep the garrulous ones from monopolizing the meeting.

One last word. Avoid time consuming meetings when you can. Some industry and association meetings, for instance, may be a political must, but you don't have to go yourself. Perhaps somebody else stands to learn more or contribute more to the meeting than you can. Perhaps you could get a better return on your time investment by being elsewhere. Appearance at the wrong meetings can rob you of precious time and energy.

Pace Yourself

An old Spanish proverb said "A man too busy to take care of his health is like a mechanic too busy to take care of his tools." Pace yourself. You have a lot to accomplish in a life-time. It is the total amount you accomplish that counts—not what you accomplish in one day or one year.

You will be in management a long time. A certain amount of pacing will be needed. Batteries need to be recharged. Fresh viewpoints must be developed. Opportunities must be attacked with vigor.

Hard work is all right. Hard work is often good for you if you enjoy it, but only if it is without conflict or emotional stress. There's no need to work yourself up to a frenzy or to get so involved that you fail to see the humor in life. Business isn't an end in itself. There is much more to life.

Watch out for alcohol. Drink if you like, but pass it up when you feel like doing so. The devil with the guy who thinks you *ought* to have a few drinks. If you prefer tomato juice, order it.

If you don't *crave* alcohol it's okay to have a drink when you feel like it. If you start to really *need* it, however, you may be headed for trouble. Like so much else, alcohol is okay in moderation but bad in extremes. Many men who would have gone to the top were knocked out by their drinking habits.

Get some exercise. Exercise is much better for sleeping than are sleeping pills.

Learn to say "no" once in a while. You can't get involved in everything people ask you to give your time to.

Take vacations, weekends, and days off. You will have to do it one way or the other—you will enjoy it much more on the golf course than in a sick bed. You will be able to accomplish more each year by working eleven months than you can by working twelve months.

In a physical kind of job where one uses his muscles it is easy to relax them at night. In a job where you think all day you may find it hard to relax because you keep on thinking after you get home. A couple of interests and hobbies of a physical nature could be a great help.

Executive health and productivity are inseparable.

Don't Play the Clown

Everyone likes a happy guy. Everyone prefers to work with an optimistic, enthusiastic, and pleasant person, a man with a sense of humor. People like clowns too. Clowns draw thousands to the circus each year.

Nobody likes to *work* with a clown, however. They may appear to laugh with him at sales meetings or the annual convention, but chances are they are more likely to be laughing *at* him.

One of the most capable men I have known in business was kept from rising to the top because of the habit of laughing at almost everything that occurred about him. He appeared to be having one heck of a good time no matter what the business situation seemed to be. Actually he was a serious guy but some-how thought he ought to be jolly. Nobody ever took him seri-ously and nobody gave him the responsibility he was techni-cally capable of handling.

Be pleasant, but don't play the clown. If you are nervous about something, don't cover it with a silly out of place laugh. Build the reputation as a serious no-nonsense kind of manager.

Don't joke or make light of people's personal problems—no matter how trivial they may seem to you. If it relates to people it is important to those it concerns. When you deal with people you must make decisions about them. They know it and they want you to give all the thought and care to your decisions about them. A light-hearted manager may gaily hire, transfer, and fire, but to the person involved, the situation is terribly important. Treat it as such.

As a manager, you must assume a sober and thoughtful style. Humor is a wonderful thing, but display it tastefully. Men do not like to entrust their economic lives to clowning managers.

If It's Connected to Business, It Is Business

Your path to success will be strewn with obstacles and oppor-tunities. You will become involved with what to all intents and purposes appear to be parties and social affairs. People will seem to be having a good time and will appear to be relaxed.

By all means enjoy the pleasanter parts of business life. Relax too at affairs of this kind. They are meant for some kind of re-laxation from the steady grind of an annual business or similar program. *But they are not parties!*

Once you say to yourself "this is great. I'm going to have a great time at this party," you're dead. If it is at all connected to business it *is* business. Others are watching you and judging you as a business executive, not as a party livener. They see you only through the eyes of business associates.

Even during the most relaxed and seemingly social occasions, avoid deviations from accepted business behavior. At almost every annual convention or important company affair I have seen at least one person make a big fool of himself by getting drunk, telling jokes that are way off color, or otherwise acting like the kind of guy you wouldn't want to entrust with a hot dog stand.

Affairs of this kind are opportunities for you to get to know your associates. They help to set a better climate for accomplishing business goals. They are opportunities to show that you have broader interests, are an interesting person, and a nice guy to be with—in addition to being a darn good business executive.

Don't forget for one moment that you are working. If you feel like having a party, go somewhere else. While you are at a company affair, or with business associates, you are *at work*. Forgetting this very important fact could cost you hundreds of thousands of dollars in your business lifetime.

Raise the Morale

Maintain a high state of morale and enthusiasm in your organization. Keep an eye to how people really feel about getting things done.

There are several things you should pay particular attention to in order to keep up a high degree of enthusiasm and morale.

Set high performance requirements. Base rewards on performance. Everyone likes to be part of a big league outfit, part of a winning team. Demand the best of everyone—including yourself.

Make it possible for each person to get a sense of satisfaction out of his present work, rather than have each job regarded merely as a step in the promotion ladder. *You* work hard only because you enjoy what you are doing. You would never work well at something you didn't enjoy. Make it possible for people to enjoy what *they* are doing. Show them how it relates to the bigger picture. Present them with the kind of challenges they can meet and the kind of obstacles they can overcome. They *want* to do a better job, if only you would help them to do it.

In making supervisory or management appointments, regard *integrity* as the one absolute requirement. This is the one quality a man has to bring with him. He cannot be expected to acquire it after he joins you. Your people would forgive you for anything else, but they will never forgive you for placing over them a man without integrity.

Focus on people's strengths—on what they can do, rather than what they cannot do. Help them to build on what they *can* do.

Never question *who* is right instead of *what* is right. The *what* is always more important than the *who*.

To ask who is right encourages subordinates to play safe and to play politics. It encourages them to cover up when a mistake has been made rather than to look for corrective action. It demoralizes them.

Talk about the ideas, concepts, and suggestions, not about *whose* ideas or suggestions they were. This is especially true if *you* thought of it (or think you thought of it). Let the other guy think it was his idea if he wants to.

Accept victories humbly and defeats philosophically. *Both* are behind you as soon as they have occurred. Look forward to what is next.

TFTT in Management

In my earlier book, *The Power of Enthusiastic Selling*, I talked about the use of the "Twenty-Five Top Target" technique for finding new business. The same idea holds true for management. The Twenty-Five Top Target technique could help you to get more accomplished.

It isn't what you do that will determine your success as a business executive, it is what you *accomplish*. Never forget that!

List the most important tasks. Get to as many of the really important things as you possibly can. You may not get to all of the objectives or tasks you have listed in a particular week or a particular month because of interruptions and unexpected developments, but you will have worked on the more important opportunities because they were at the top of your list. In that way you will earn more money and will get more done.

You have got to know your targets. You must know exactly what you are shooting at. (How else can you measure accomplishments?)

Pick your specific targets. Use the Twenty-Five Top Target technique. The number is arbitrary. It could be more than twenty-five targets or fewer. Review the list frequently. Situations change. Opportunities change. Make sure you are going after the most realistic and most profitable objectives you can under current circumstances.

Go after those objectives you are most likely to reach. Concentrate on those areas that have the greatest promise for success. Set the targets where you can accomplish more for your company and yourself.

Set priorities to all you do. Do the most important first. You will never get to finish all you want to do, but you will get to what is most important and most productive.

Make Sure They Remember You

They will remember, if you do. They will remember if you approach them with confidence and ease. Speak to people as if it is the most natural thing in the world for you to be speaking to *them*.

They will remember if you treat each and every one as a different individual.

Make sure you remember them, though. People's names are important to the people they belong to. Keep records of the names of people you meet. Review those records when you are likely to see them again. It often goes further back than that, however. It often goes back to the need to learn the names in the first place.

Special training or exercise is the secret of memory improvement. The more you use your powers of concentration and recall, the more effective they will become. Let's discuss a few suggestions as to how to remember a name and a face.

The first rule is to *concentrate*. Know that it *can* be done. Give it all you have for the few moments you hear the name and attempt to implant it in your memory. Memory can be strengthened and developed by exercise. Get your mind in the habit of remembering anything you want it to. Test your memory. Memorize all the phone numbers you can, titles of books, important statistics, the names of the people you meet. Learn to observe and concentrate. What was the foreman wearing the last time you spoke to him? What color dress is your secretary wearing? What color tie do *you* have on today? (Don't look.)

There are three basic steps which will help you to remember names:

1. *Get the name clearly.* If you don't get it right in the first place, you will never remember it. Be sure you know how to pronounce it and how to spell it. If you are not sure, *ask*. People are complimented when you take enough interest in them to want to know how to spell their names.

2. *Use the name at once.* "That seems to be a great opportunity, Mr. Hansel." Use the name at once and use it often. The first few moments of concentration and reinforcement by repetition are most important.

3. *Write it down.* Write the name down as soon as you can. Scribble it on an envelope or a scrap of paper. Get it down in writing just as soon as you can. If you are in conversation with several people, take advantage of the moments when one of the

group seems to be addressing another member. Jot down all the names. You've just *got* to remember.

When you meet a number of people in a group, as you will quite often, and the introductions are made rather hurriedly, here is what you do:

1. If you know it will be a large group, arrive early. Get there before there are too many. You will meet fewer people at a time and will get the benefit of hearing names repeated as the later arrivals are introduced.

2. Repeat the names if you can, out loud in your conversations, or mentally to yourself. If you have forgotten some, ask the host, one of the members of the group, or the persons themselves. Show that you want to remember them.

3. Slow down the introductions if necessary. Repeat each person's name as he is introduced. Shake hands. Look at him. Regard him as the most important and only person in the world for that moment. Determine that you will know and remember his name.

4. After you leave, go over each name. Jot them down. Make a mental picture of each person. Jot down outstanding characteristics that will help you to remember.

In a Nutshell

Set out to do even more than your goals for you've got to be *sure* you accomplish what you set out to do. Go to the man at the top when you want things done. Keep up the drive that gets results. Plan as imaginatively and boldly as your mind permits and act with deliberation within that plan. Demand the maximum return on all that you do. Think for yourself and build on your strengths.

Top target thinking, effective use of meetings, a sense of humor in a clownless way, and a balanced approach to business leadership will make you a pro.

You're in it for success and you're in it for life. Make it a long one.

17

MANAGEMENT
IN A CHANGING WORLD

What about the future? What will we as man-
agers need to be and need to do to provide leadership in a world
which is changing faster and faster? What kind of changes could
we foresee? How will this affect the role of the business
manager?

In the past twenty years the tempo of change has become
explosive, producing greater transformation than in the previous 2,000 years. The rate of change will accelerate even more
in the next twenty years.

The prosperity of any business will depend on the performance of its managers. Business decisions require a longer and
longer time-span for their fruition. Since no one can foresee
the future with great degree of accuracy the managers of tomorrow will have to be men who adjust quickly to changing
environments and who can make decisions and follow through
as opportunities develop.

Look Beyond the Present

Prepare yourself for the tasks of tomorrow. Think always of
what will be needed in the years ahead and what you should be

doing *now* to prepare yourself for leadership in that future. Think of these needs in terms of your own future, your own business, and your own job.

Many managers tend to retreat to the familiar. They tend to do those things with which they are more familiar and more comfortable. Just as a good General advances, so does a good Executive. Adjust your thinking to the fact that you will have to keep adjusting your thinking. Look beyond your present job. You won't see the forest for the trees if you keep your nose on the grindstone.

You may have heard this one but it illustrates the point of concentrating so hard on the present narrow task that little is accomplished: "Keep your shoulder to the wheel, your nose to the grindstone, and your eye on the ball—now try to work in that position!"

The Kind of Management Tomorrow Needs

We live in an era of explosive technological achievement. Inventions of our scientific age will continue to effect, in increasing tempo, the lives of all.

The economy, prodded by world competition and heavy government spending, will grow at an accelerated rate. A by-product of these large expenditures will be new technologies which will pave the way for new consumer industries. Whole industries will become outmoded while others blossom and expand.

Industry will be swamped in an avalanche of paper as the needs for record keeping and documentation increase. The men who can get things done will be in greater demand and shorter supply. Management will be faced with more strenuous requirements.

The top will more and more be filled by men who have been trained to *think*. The rate of obsolescence and the atmosphere of continuous change will grow, speed up, and become more critical. It will bring faster technological and organizational changes.

Developments in data processing and information technology will change the job of management. Managers of the 70's and 80's may need to be more scientifically and technically qualified. Available knowledge, technology, and a faster moving pace will require more team management. No individual could possibly keep up with the geometrically progressing changes.

Schools may need to train one group as specialists, another as middle management, and another for top management. The apprentice system as we know it today—going up through the ranks—may become obsolete for the man who does not prepare himself for the top right from the start.

The Age of Automation

Automation will employ more people who are highly skilled and highly trained. The manager's responsibility and competence, his vision, his capacity to choose between alternate risks, his economic knowledge, his ability to manage managers, and his competence in making decisions will be greatly increased by the data which automation will make available to him.

There will be an increasing dependence on staff people as the reservoir for top management positions, because it will be the staff people brought up in an advanced automated information technology that management will have to rely on more and more.

Time-span for the fruition and proving out of decisions will continue to lengthen. Advanced information processing techniques will be relied on more and more to reduce the risk and the unknown from management decisions.

Automation as such is a continuation of a process that started many years ago. By continuing to profit from the benefits of new technology while solving the adjustment problems that change always brings, the managers of tomorrow can help to lead the nation into even greater productivity and wealth.

R & D * in Marketing

Innovation is a slow process. New concepts and new products evolve slowly. Many companies owe their leadership today to activities started more than ten or twenty years ago. Conversely, any company which stops innovating is on its way to bankruptcy. Any *person* who ceases to innovate is on his way to decay.

Innovation, like much else discussed in this book, applies to small business as well as big. No business can stand still. It either goes ahead or lags behind.

What the business is and what it will become is not determined by the producer but by the *consumer.* The business you are in is determined by the want or need the customer satisfies when he buys your product. Look at your business—and your job—from the point of view of the marketplace. That alone will help you to forecast and prepare for the management needs of tomorrow.

It is the customer, who through being willing to pay for a product or service, converts economic resources into wealth. What the customer considers as good value determines what a business is and will become. It is the customer who decides how a business will prosper.

The customer is the foundation of a business. He keeps it in existence. He alone gives employment.

It takes a lifetime to learn about the world in which we live and the people with whom we work. We never learn enough about the market in which we sell, about the forces of competition, the pressures of government and public opinion, and the variability of the human brain. Prediction beyond a few weeks

---

* Research and Development.

is one of the toughest jobs we have. Yet this is precisely what we as managers must do.

Only a management attitude attuned to constant change and adjustment could survive this kind of world. Decisions concerning the future will always remain anticipations. The odds will always be against their being right. You must at all times, therefore, allow room for changes.

Changing Times

Research, engineering, and marketing will move closer. It will more and more be difficult to tell where an idea started, where the concept moved from one stage to the other, and when it actually hit the market. Development will go on right in the customers' plants, in company field offices, or in company service centers.

Customers will start to use the product as it is being developed and as it is being refined. This will assure concepts and equipment that will give maximum customer satisfaction, will be engineered and produced with the greatest economy, and best of all will avoid having to go through re-engineering and de-bugging every time it moves from one stage to the other. The problem of finding drawbacks as a machine or process emerges from the research laboratories into engineering, or finding bugs that were not anticipated as it goes from engineering into production, or production to the market place, will disappear.

This is the kind of world the manager of tomorrow must prepare for. One of variation and change, one of dynamic growth!

The People Side of Changes

Whenever we talk about planned change, we talk of people. To introduce changes as if people were not involved is to doom the change effort to defeat.

People fear changes. It undermines their security. In making a change make sure you get the active support, advice, and participation of the people affected.

Keep them with you all the way. From the realization and understanding of the problem and factors involved to the steps in arriving at the solution. Unless you do this all your foresight and your ability to see change will mean absolutely nothing.

The Priceless Ingredient

Each age calls for different characteristics and strengths. Most successful men are children of the age in which they live, people with a gift for seizing on what the age had to offer them. There is one characteristic or ingredient that will be vital for the manager of tomorrow, and that is *integrity*.

The integrity required will be even greater than that needed today. Under new technology and the impact of decisions, their time-span and great risks will be so serious as to require that the manager put the common good above his own self interest.

The impact on people will be so decisive as to demand that genuine principles be put above expediency. Management will be so complex that only a highly principled, highly secure, and far-seeing person could survive.

The impact of management actions on the economy will be so far reaching that society will hold the manager accountable. The manager of tomorrow will need to root every action and every decision on the bedrock of principles. He will have to lead through knowledge, competence, skill, vision, courage, responsibility, and *integrity*.

R & D in People

Millions of dollars are being poured into the development of new products, and this is all very good. It is *people* however who will determine how great a business or a nation will become. It is people-development that business of the future may start to pour millions into, for in that way only will we come closer to realizing the potential that most people have far and above what they are using today.

Development of managers of the future will require more and more attention. More and more help will be asked and accepted from social scientists, psychologists, and others who could help in developing what is still perhaps the greatest untapped source—people.

Better means will be found to develop leaders and to appraise the younger ones as they come along. Fresh thinking on this problem must be stimulated. New techniques and principles for corporate growth must be found. Industry has gone a long way, but there is an even brighter path ahead and infinitely more that can be accomplished.

Management must spend more on social sciences in the Research and Development efforts. With so much to be gained from the development of more effective ways to help people unleash tremendous stores of energy and ability, some of the monies going into product research should perhaps be placed into people research. The cash dividends of such pioneering may well eclipse the possible returns on product research. The very survival of the corporate way of life may in fact depend on it.

Nothing Stays the Same

"Facts" or reality is a process of continuous change. It is a never-ending series of changes in ourselves and the world around us. No two things are exactly alike. No one person or thing stays the same.

History does *not* repeat itself. The past is gone forever. Those who seek to hold onto the past can only disintegrate as the past they cherish recedes further and further into oblivion.

Change is one of the few certainties of life. An increasing premium will be placed on those who help people and organizations to adjust to change.

Change can defeat only those who do not expect it, only those, who in planning their lives, leave it out of consideration.

Will You Be Ready?

If you were made President of your company next week, could you handle the job? Would you have convictions as to where you should lead your company? Will you have a clear picture of what you and your company ought to be preparing for? It takes special skill, training, and discipline, to see *before-hand* what everybody says was obvious *after* somebody else thought of it. Monday morning quaterbacks are never given the ball to carry.

The race is to the swift. The prize will be awarded for endurance, persistence, foresight, and steady pace.

In a Nutshell

The speed of change increases geometrically. To maintain a postion of leadership you must foresee change, plan for it, and adjust to it. Innovation will remain the lifeblood of organizations and of the people who run them.

Corporate activity will move closer to the market place with changes more and more determined by the buying public.

People development will become more critical. Tremendous power for positive accomplishment will be unleashed from the producers of tomorrow's economy. Most of all, however, honesty and integrity will become even more vital as guiding principles in a world of increasing tempo and change.

18

THE RESPONSIBILITY
OF LEADERSHIP

Leadership carries with it a number of responsi-
bilities as well as privileges. Abuse the responsibilities and the
privileges will be lost.

The more business leaders can personally demonstrate the
best qualities of the managerial mind, and the more they can
make it a living reality, the more meaningful will be the efforts
of everyone in adding to the stature of management. As a member of management you can do much to fulfill the wants and
the needs of so many.

For Power or Performance?

If the reason you want to get into management is so that you
could have and exert *power,* forget it. You will never make it to
the top. Your job will be *to get things done,* not to show how
terrible or how powerful you can be. The day is gone when you
could get people to do things because *you* want them to or because you control the carrot and the stick. You will get things
done *only if the people who are to do them understand and
want to see them done.*

There is no denying that power goes with position. When used for the good of the group, when used wisely, power is a valuable tool. When used for personal gratification, however, power is destructive.

Men and women deserve and ultimately will demand the growth, development, and expression of the non-material side of their beings. They expect and will demand to be treated as human equals. Business exists for man's sake. Man does not exist for the sake of business. One of the functions of business is to give opportunity for individual development through the better organization of human relationships. Businessmen can lead the world.

Power carries responsibility. Responsibility increases with position and power. Take the responsibility to heart.

The People Around You

No one can be a leader unless he has followers who want to follow. Your goals and those of the people working for you must be the same. The better you integrate all the goals, the more successful you will be.

People want to participate in the decisions that directly affect their work. The creative leader must help his people to so plan their work. Give them a stake in accomplishing the goals. Reward them for what *you* would like to be rewarded. One man pushing the oar in the opposite direction could make the difference between winning the race or finishing last.

The more effective groups are those where the atmosphere is informal, where everyone participates.

To motivate your people to peak performance you must set and enforce on yourself high standards of ethics and high standards of performance.

You can't fool them.

What you are thinking will come through to your associates

and others. Those you like and understand will normally feel the same way about you.

Titles and names are important to people. "Hey, boy" or "you there" won't get much done for you. He has a name. Use it. Show that you consider him important enough to have learned his name.

If you treat a man as he is he will remain as he is. If you treat him as he *could be,* he will grow. Your power and opportunity for helping people and getting things done are great. Don't fumble it.

The People You Pick

You could do only so much by yourself. To carry out your responsibilities a lot will depend on the people you pick for leadership positions.

All the practices and techniques of good management will not build a success-destined organization if you don't pick the right people for management positions. The final proof of your sincerity, seriousness, and uncompromising emphasis on integrity of character will be the type of people you promote or appoint. It is *character* through which leadership is exercised. It is character that sets the example.

Make sure the man *wants* to be appointed. Some people are actually driven into panic and disappointment because they feel psychologically forced to accept a promotion when it is offered. It is the socially acceptable thing to do. The responsibility for seeing the situation as it is and for acting wisely is *yours.* Weigh carefully, the people you pick.

The people who constitute management in the United States hold their jobs as managers of the American economy because the people of America still trust management to operate the economy. A lot depends on your building further confidence in American business managers.

The Power of Your Word

Everything the boss says is long remembered. The words you use are powerful. Use them carefully.

Treat a promise as a contract in writing. Be slower to make promises but keep those you make. Be careful though, because employees will hear what they want to hear. If you don't intend it to be a promise, be sure they clearly understand.

If you can't keep a promise don't pretend it wasn't made. Tell him as soon as you know why you cannot do what you hoped you would be able to do. Do what you can to alleviate whatever disadvantage your promise may have put him into.

Enthusiasm is a wonderful thing, but when it comes to promises, don't let it run away from you. Stick to the facts, even when they aren't pleasant. Be realistic. Don't paint too rosy a picture —you may be hung with it.

Be especially careful when you talk to people about their hopes and ambitions. They will remember every word you say. More than that, they will frequently let their imagination enlarge on your remarks, so don't make it worse by saying more than you honestly could. Wishful thinking has a way of distorting facts. It is relatively easy to turn a "maybe" of yours into an iron-clad promise if that's what he wanted to hear.

When you do promise anything, move heaven and earth to deliver the goods. Don't back out of a promise because it becomes inconvenient for you to follow through. A promise is a contract. Live up to it.

Your Stake in the Community

Business leaders have a major stake in economics, politics, and human society. They are interrelated. What is good for all should be a basic consideration. Nothing should be done in business or otherwise which goes contrary to the common good.

Because we have a major stake in the future of the nation and because we are equipped by training and experience to think and to lead, we must take an active part in what goes on about us. We have a responsibility to speak up and say what we think.

Incentives, income, profits, rewards—call it what you will—are the motivating factors behind all achievement.

The profit system is something to be proud of. The anticipation of reward is what has built the nation—its railroads, its communication lines, its airlines, its food processing plants, and everything else we use and enjoy. The profit system has given people a better way of life. It has provided more jobs and better products. It has enabled those who *can* to produce more for the benefit of all. Reward a man for what he does and he will do much more. Try to get something out of him without paying him for it and you will find there is little to get.

Take an active part in your community and its politics. Make your thoughts known and help your community to thrive and grow.

Help if you can with volunteer work, such as community drives. You will find it intriguing and you will find it contributes materially to your breadth of knowledge and managerial skills.

Don't accept honorary titles or officerships in any business, social or political organization unless you intend to at least be active enough to keep abreast of what is going on. Make sure this is the kind of organization you want to lend your name to. Be sure that those who support the organization because they see *you* are associated with it are not disappointed or shocked by some later disclosure or scandal. This kind of thing has happened before. Don't let it happen to you.

Management, its competence, its integrity, and its performance, will be decisive to the free world in the years ahead. The demands on management will be rising steadily and steeply.

The uneasy peace which we have been living through puts

heavy economic burdens on our nation, which only continuous economic advances can make possible. It requires ability to satisfy the country's military needs while building at the same time an expanding economy. It demands an unprecedented ability of the economy to shift back and forth between peacetime and defense production. This demand, on the satisfaction of which our survival may well depend, is a demand on the ability of modern management.

The responsibility of management is decisive for the public standing and public image of business, its success and its status. It is decisive for the very future of our economic and social system and the survival of the private ownership, profit-oriented, system. If you understand this and believe it, accept as your responsibility the task of strengthening the system and protecting it from irresponsible abuse.

Participating in community affairs additionally has a special personal value to you in your executive development program. Not only will you be contributing to better government, but you will find that your activities help you to develop abilities to get things done through people. These are *voluntary* associates you will be working with. You will have absolutely no artificial authority or power over them. Whatever they do for you and with you they will do because they *want* to—because you make them want to—not because they have to. Participation in community affairs will give you management experience and exposure to the type of problems you will run into in managing any kind of organization.

Ethics Help Accomplish Business Goals

"Don't be a fool," you may hear "you can't afford to be honest in business. Business is a matter of dog eat dog. It is the one who knows how to lie and cheat who gets ahead."

Nothing could be further from the truth. The ones who get

to the top are by far men of high moral fibre, men with a high sense of service and responsibility, men who are honest with themselves and their associates. The kind of advantage they seek out of each transaction is a *mutual* advantage. They know that only when both parties to any transaction gain from the association is there a chance for real progress for either party.

Dishonesty has prevented some brilliant and otherwise capable people from reaching the top. I have known men who could have become presidents of their companies if they devoted as much energy to getting the job done as they did to cheating other people. Their subordinates had no respect for them and did not help them.

Honesty pays, and it pays well!

The kind of man you are will determine the kind of people who will be working for you and the kind of organization you can create. It will determine in fact the kind of customers you have and the character of your business.

The question of morality and ethics are interwoven with the matter of corporate and personal image. They have more to do with business success than most people realize.

The personal behavior of the boss is important. Nobody wants a clown for a manager. Leadership carries with it a solemn responsibility. Men may kid and joke about travelling salesmen or after-hours activities, but don't let it fool you. Most of them are just trying to pass the time away in some facetious conversation. Most people have high moral standards and will judge you by those standards.

You can't afford to stray from that personal image. I have known executives who have pursued loose personal standards but in every case their actions have held them back from a more successful career.

Your personal philosophy and personal ethics must be an integral part of your business philosophy and ethics. Be proud to live by them.

Here are some simple guidelines:

1. The interests of your company must be placed before your private interests. If what you are about to do will conflict with one or the other, do what is best for your company or get out. You cannot succeed if your efforts do not help your company to succeed.

2. Your duty to society must be placed even above duty to your company or yourself. What you do must not be harmful to the society in which you live. If it hurts the community it will eventually hurt your company. Again, if you cannot avoid hurting society by what you are about to do, even though it is what you think your company wants, change your company's thinking or get out. Don't compromise this one unless you want to compromise your future and yourself. Compromise yourself and you will never succeed.

3. If you are not sure but think there may be a conflict of interests, let your company know what you are doing. Keep it in the open. If your interests and the company's interests are involved, let the company know what you are doing, even if you don't think there is a conflict. You will feel better that way and you might avoid a lot of hardship.

Managers must become increasingly conscious of how they are responsible to the company, to society, and to their own selves. The successful manager is a serious student of people, group behavior, experiment, and change. New values, new goods, new distributions, new ideas, are constant challenges that can be met only within the framework of high moral standards.

Management Is a Responsibility, Not a Goal

Many aspiring executives foolishly look to a management assignment as the culmination of all of their efforts, as an end to be accomplished. They look to it as a reward, rather than a challenge. They see a management job as one where you sit behind a desk and adjudicate whatever is brought before you. Managers and executives are people who get things done. Unless you *know* that, and unless you step into the job with a sense of challenge and a determination to get things done, you will never make it.

At any point of business life, if you feel you have arrived, you are on the way down. The moment you stop getting better, you start to lose ground.

Human relations will be one of the greatest challenges to your resourcefulness and foresight. Everyone wants some part in shaping the scheme of things in which he is involved. It will be *your* job to see that he gets that sense of participation.

People *like* to work. See to it that their jobs offer them more than just a chance to earn a living. See to it that they get pleasure out of the job itself. See to it that you release the mass of energy that is imprisoned within unstimulated and unmotivated workers, and waiting to burst forth with a tremendous surge in corporate production. Eliminate the incalculable loss which an economy suffers because people lack interest in their work.

Yours is a responsibility for seeing that your business and your organization fills peoples' needs, provides satisfaction, and leads the way, in addition to the responsibility for making a profit. Yours is the responsibility for seeing that high values guide you and your subordinates in making decisions. Values, you will find, can be viewed independently of profits. Profits will usually follow, if the values you live by reflect a high degree of management responsibility and leadership.

A business does not exist in isolation. It exists in a society that includes hospitals, schools, churches, government agencies, and other groups and individuals. Business must operate within the general beliefs and accepted codes of conduct of this society.

Wide deviations could jeopardize the very existence of any business organization in the society.

If private enterprise does not meet the essential demands which our nation places upon its economy, private management will lose the job of managing the economy. The stakes are very high indeed.

To survive and grow, every business enterprise must have an underlying philosophy of service to the public.

In a Nutshell

You have a serious responsibility as a manager of the economy and a leader of people. You have a responsibility to promote the kind of people others want to follow, the kind who will get things done. Your word is often a matter of business life and feeling of participation to those who work for you. Treat your people and what you promise with deep respect.

The responsibility for management in many parts of the world have been taken out of private hands and have been assumed by political powers. The result by far has been poverty, decay, and enslavement. The people of America, however, have continued to entrust economic growth in the hands of private management and personal leadership. It's up to you to assure that that confidence will continue to be well placed.

19

KEEP GROWING

Executive growth is a matter of discipline. It is the result of systematic and persistent improvement. Business management is the one profession where a man could keep improving and where a man does not reach his peak until he is well in the sixties. Any man who stops learning and growing is selling himself short. He is robbing himself of tremendous opportunities.

Executives don't just happen—they are carefully developed!

You Can't Let Well Enough Alone

The great danger to a person or an organization is complacency, especially the complacency that follows success.

No individual, no company, and no organization can stand still. You either move ahead or fall back. You get better or you degenerate. You learn more or forget what you know. You become sharper and more capable or dull and mediocre.

Competition never gives up. The economy is dynamic. Others are constantly pushing ahead. To stand still is to fall behind.

All products have a limited life. New developments come up to replace them. Forms of corporate organization and philosophy of management will continue to change. To stop learning and to stop adjusting to changing needs is to stop growing. You might not recognize it right away but without a shadow of a doubt you will wake up one day to find yourself out of step with the times.

Planning and thinking must always be tied to the future. Ask yourself at all times what will things be like five years from today? What will we need? What action will put me in a better position when that time comes?

History has shown, again and again, that the rich and the fat are overtaken by the lean and the hungry. You cannot afford to be complacent. You must run scared. You must in every way continue to grow. You owe it to yourself, and you owe it to your company, to spend some of your time and effort in self-devel-opment.

Your Personal Curriculum

All management development is self-development. Only *you* can work out the training program that is best for your needs, your strengths, and your ambitions.

All education is self-education. A teacher cannot really teach. He can only help others to learn.

Learning is most efficient when goals are clear. Goals which you yourself impose are the most powerful of all. You work harder to accomplish them.

Learning requires a mental flexibility that accepts change. Resistance to change will block effective learning. Learning requires that you *seek* criticism. Lots of what people tell you *now* contains constructive criticism if only you would be smart enough to listen.

Learn in every way you can. Learn by reading, lectures, discussion, analysis of your own experiences, feed-back from those you work with, experimentation with new ideas, role-playing, and lots and lots of practice.

Develop that extra ability and extra knowledge that will in-

deed give you power—the power to get things done for others
and for yourself. Develop an interest in everything. It's all relevant—from a hippopotamus to a microbe. It all relates to you
and your life.

In setting up your curriculum or program ask what it is that
your boss has to know. What must he be able to do? What about
his associates? What do others at the level above have to be able
to accomplish?

The answers to those questions could help you make up the
curriculum of your own management development program.
Remember, however, that you don't always move up to your
boss's job. That is just a guide. You might move across organizational lines to another department or to a newly created position. Your training must be broader than that if your opportunities are to be unlimited.

While we are talking of training and of growing let me say
this about college. Get a college education if you possibly can.
It will improve your chances by about one thousand percent.
In many companies a college diploma is a requirement for ad-
mission to the management group. Most men in the management group have college degrees. That is the competition you
will be up against.

Go even beyond that. Your training and your education must
be on a broader basis. To get to the top you will need to understand more than is taught in college. More and more the top
executive is a person with broad intellectual and cultural interests. Business is becoming more complex. It is tied to social
development, world events, government relationships, and financial considerations. The men who are going to lead a business will need to keep on learning.

Mindstretching

The past is gone—think ahead. A man's mind could be
stretched. There is more and more evidence that I.Q.'s can con-

tinue to grow. Use, challenge, and stimulation can make a man's effective intelligence grow. Use of more of the intellectual power which people already have can bring miraculous results. Every time you exercise your imagination, your reason, and your judgment, you strengthen these powers. Every time you stretch your mind, you grow.

People learn from experience. Experience comes only with experimentation. Keep experimenting, keep adjusting, and keep preparing for the ever-changing future. *Create* new opportunities for experience and experimentation. *Force* yourself to grow.

Join success-oriented groups. Attend top business schools on a graduate or special course basis. Attend seminars of the American Management Association and similar groups. Attend special courses and programs given by professional groups, such as the Sales and Marketing Executives Clubs, The Controllers' Institute, and others. Be active in your industry association groups and in progressive community programs.

Make new contacts and renew stimulating old ones. Meet as many people as you can. You could *never* know too many people. It is easy to make friends. People worth knowing want to know more people.

Be a man of the future. Think in terms of what the future will be like and what its needs will be. You will get ahead and stay ahead if you *think* ahead.

Pull Way Out in Front

There is lots of competition in business, but it is best handled by making yourself better than the next man, not by trying to tear the other man down.

Whatever energies you exert in trying to protect your job are better spent in preparing yourself for the next job.

The day you receive your promotion and step into a new

job is the day you should start training the best men under you to do your job. The more they know about your job, the more time you will have to learn the assignments above you. Help the other fellow to grow and spend *your* energy growing even faster.

A man never really leaves a position to his successor precisely as he received it from his predecessor. He will have added a little or subtracted from his duties; he will have changed directions at least slightly; and he may have actually set records difficult for anyone else to match, let alone improve upon. Resolve that *you* will leave each job better than you found it. Resolve that you will have made a major contribution to every assignment that comes your way.

Keep learning and keep growing. Devote as much time and energy as you can to the problem of the future. The future arrives with increasing rapidity. Except in unusual circumstances, do not go into the office on weekends. Use the time to relax and to work on longer range more important problems —not on office details. Use the time to study and learn about the things that will make you even more important to yourself and to your company.

As soon as you have thoroughly learned your job ask for more responsibility. You can't afford to waste time and you can't let yourself become rusty. A good athlete is always in training. He is always pushing to peak performance. A good executive does the same.

A Philosophy and a Pitch

How to Motivate and Persuade People is based on the philosophy that by helping others and getting them to participate, *you* will grow. It is hoped that there were many things in this book that will help you to become a more effective executive and will help you in your personal and business growth.

If you feel that what you read in this book was helpful and if you feel it could be helpful to others, practice this management philosophy by recommending the book to others.

And Now to Sum It All Up

Set your sights very high and far ahead. Develop the power and techniques to drive you to the top. Continue to feed that power with positive team-inspiring enthusiasm.

Set and continue to re-set your goals and your plans for reaching those goals. Start to accomplish *now*. Yesterday is gone and tomorrow is late. Work relentlessly to accomplish your present goals.

To get more done you'll have to work with and through more people. Pick the winners. Give them a feeling of participation. Motivate them to outpace and outproduce the competition.

Step way out in front. Raise the standards way up high. There's much dependent on what you think and what you do.

Develop the strength of mental flexibility. This fast changing world will quicken its pace. Stay way ahead of the changes which are sure to come.

If you believe in yourself and the people around you, learn well the principles of business and personal success, stick to it with a sincere, dedicated, and positive persistency, you *will* reach the goals you have set.

INDEX